Moral Dimensions

Moral
Dimensions

PERMISSIBILITY, MEANING, BLAME

T. M. Scanlon

Belknap Press of Harvard University Press
Cambridge, Massachusetts London, England

First Harvard University Press paperback edition, 2010

Library of Congress Cataloging-in-Publication Data

Scanlon, Thomas.
    Moral dimensions : permissibility, meaning, blame / T. M. Scanlon.
        p. cm.
    Includes bibliographical references and index.
    ISBN 978-0-674-03178-4 (cloth: alk. paper)
    ISBN 978-0-674-05745-6 (pbk.)
    1. Ends and means.   2. Intention.   3. Blame—Moral and ethical
aspects.   I. Title.

BJ84.E5S23 2008
170'.42—dc22   2008016218

For Lucy

Contents

Preface   *ix*

Introduction   1

1   The Illusory Appeal of Double Effect   8

2   The Significance of Intent   37

3   Means and Ends   89

4   Blame   122

Notes   *217*

Bibliography   *239*

Index   *243*

Preface

This book has its origins in discussions at meetings of the Society for Ethical and Legal Philosophy. The significance of the distinction between intended and merely foreseen consequences was a recurrent topic over the course of twenty years, and a subject of strong disagreement within the group. I myself was always torn. The distinction seemed to fit well with my judgments of right and wrong in many cases—better than any other account I could think of. But I was unable to explain why this difference in an agent's attitudes should have such moral importance, and unable to defend the distinction against the counterexamples that Judith Thomson and others would raise. Further discussions with Judy and others in 1996, about whether we should rely on intent as an important factor in the argument of an amicus curiae brief concerning assisted suicide, intensified my feeling of being intellectually whipsawed on this issue—drawn one way by the apparent ability of double effect to explain particular cases, and in the opposite direction by my inability to defend it as a general principle.

Hoping to come to some settled opinion on the question, I made it the topic of my graduate seminar at Harvard in the spring of 1999. I was fortunate to have an outstanding group of students in that seminar, who were willing to work through the extensive and difficult literature on double effect and on killing and letting die. My main objectives were to understand whether the permissibility of an action can depend on whether a given harm is intended by the agent or merely foreseen as a side effect of his or her action, and, if permissibility does not depend on intent in this way, to understand why the idea that it depends on intent should seem so plausible. By the end of the semester I had come up with provisional answers to these questions, which after many revisions became Chapter 1 of this book.

My first debts of gratitude, then, are to my fellow members of the Society for Ethical and Legal Philosophy, for many years of stimulating discussions, and to the members of my Harvard seminar, for their critical acumen and their good-spirited willingness to tramp through jungles of argument in pursuit of an elusive quarry.

The first version of Chapter 1 was presented to the Joint Session of the Aristotelian Society and the Mind Association in the summer of 2000, and published as "Permissibility and

Intention I" in *Proceedings of the Aristotelian Society,* Supp. Vol. 74 (2000): 301–317. Jonathan Dancy was my co-symposiast, and his comments helped me to see some of the ways in which that article could be improved.

All four chapters of this book have been presented as lectures at many universities and have benefited from the comments I received on those occasions. In particular, Chapters 1, 2, and 4 were discussed at the New York University Colloquium in Legal, Political and Social Philosophy. The first version of Chapter 3 was the Gareth Evans Memorial Lecture at Oxford, November 16, 2004. Chapter 4 was first presented as the Jack Smart Lecture at the Australian National University in Canberra, in July 2003; later versions were given as the Seybert Lectures at the University of Pennsylvania, and as the Howison Lecture at the University of California, Berkeley. I am grateful to the audiences on all these occasions for stimulating and helpful discussion.

Derek Parfit, the most loyal friend and helpful critic one could imagine, read multiple versions of all of these chapters. His extensive comments have saved me from many errors and made the book far better than it otherwise would have been.

The book has also benefited from the comments of other friends, students, and colleagues who read or heard versions of these chapters. They include (at least) Harry Adamson, G. A. Cohen, Joshua Cohen, Tom Dougherty, Patricio Fernandez, Samuel Freeman, Jorge Garcia, Aaron Garrett, Kent Greenawalt, Paul Guyer, Pamela Hieronymi, Waheed Hussain, Aaron James, Frances Kamm, Erin Kelly, Michael Joel Kessler, Niko Kolodny, Jeff McMahan, Japa Pallikkathayil, Philip Pettit, Robert Post, Raffaele Rodogno, Samuel Scheffler,

Tommie Shelby, Seana Shiffrin, John Skorupski, Angela Smith, Robert Stalnaker, Sigrun Svavarsdottir, Dennis Thompson, Judith Thomson, Alec Walen, R. Jay Wallace, Ralph Wedgwood, and Roger Wertheimer. I thank all of them for their helpful comments and suggestions. I am grateful, as always, to my wife, Lucy, for her understanding and support.

Moral Dimensions

Introduction

The doctrine of double effect holds that an action that aims at the death of an innocent person, either as its end or as a means to its end, is always wrong. In particular, it holds that such an action cannot be justified by its good effects, such as saving the lives of a greater number of innocent people. This doctrine gains plausibility from its ability to explain some otherwise puzzling cases. For example, if the limited amount of a drug that is available could be used either to save one patient or to save five others, it is permissible to give it to the five, even though the one will die. But it would not be permissible to withhold the same drug from the same person in order to save the five others by transplanting his organs into them after he is dead. According to the doctrine of double effect, such an action would be impermissible because in the latter case, unlike in the former, one withholds the drug from the one in order to bring about the death of the one, as a means to save the five.

Similarly, many people believe that in war it can be permissible to bomb a military target even though this will also cause the deaths of some noncombatants living nearby, but that it would not be permissible to bomb the same number of noncombatants in order to hasten the end of the war by demoralizing the population. Again the doctrine of double effect seems to offer an explanation: in the latter case, but not the former, one would be aiming at the deaths of innocent people (people who pose no threat) as a means to one's end.

The ability to explain cases of this kind gives the doctrine of double effect considerable initial appeal. But it is not at all clear how an agent's intentions could determine permissibility of an action in the way that the doctrine claims. To my knowledge, no convincing theoretical explanation for it has been offered, and arguments against this idea by Judith Thomson and others have seemed to me persuasive.

If one rejects the doctrine of double effect, as I am inclined to do, then one is left with two questions. First, if this doctrine is not the correct explanation in cases like the ones I have mentioned, what is? Second, if the doctrine of double effect is mistaken, why should it seem so plausible as an explanation for these cases? What mistake underlies its appeal?

I believe that the illusory appeal of double effect arises from a confusion between two closely related forms of moral judgment, which can be based on the same moral principles. Judgments of the first kind use a principle in what I call its deliberative employment to answer a question of permissibility, whether an agent may perform an action of a certain kind.

Judgments of the second kind employ principles in their critical use, to assess the way in which an agent went about deciding what to do on a given occasion. Judgments of the latter sort depend on what the agent saw as reasons bearing on the decision about what to do. Even when the permissibility of an action does not depend on what the agent took to be reasons, it may appear to do so if judgments of these two kinds are not clearly distinguished. I present this explanation in detail in Chapter 1.

This explanation of the appeal of the doctrine of double effect depends on a particular understanding of the idea of moral permissibility, which leads to several further questions about how the disagreement between supporters and critics of the doctrine should be understood. This might be a disagreement about what determines the permissibility or impermissibility of certain actions. But the disagreement might arise instead from the fact that the parties are asking different basic questions. It might be that although many opponents of double effect are concerned with the question of permissibility, many supporters of double effect take some other moral notion, such as the idea of a good action, to be basic. If so, this raises further questions about what these different moral notions are and what grounds there are for assigning one of them rather than another a central role in our moral thinking. I raise these questions in Chapter 1, but I do not undertake to answer them, since the first question, in particular, is one that supporters of double effect are best placed to answer. I hope that my argument will lead to further discussion of this question.

Nor do I offer a single direct answer to the first of the questions I posed above: if the doctrine of double effect is not the correct explanation in cases like those I described at the outset, what is the correct explanation? My own view is that there is no single explanation for all of the cases to which the doctrine of double effect is thought to apply. The explanation of what is permissible or impermissible in transplant cases is different from what explains the difference between terror bombing and tactical bombing, and different still from the explanation of what is permissible when dealing with runaway trolleys. (I discuss these cases in Chapter 1 and Chapter 3.)

If the permissibility of an action does not depend on the agent's intentions in the way that the doctrine of double effect maintains, this leaves open the possibility that there are other ways in which permissibility does depend on intent, or on an agent's reasons for acting. In Chapter 2 I identify a number of ways in which permissibility depends on an agent's intentions, and I examine some other ways in which it may appear to depend on an agent's intentions but does not do so, at least not in a fundamental way. In the course of this investigation I develop and explore an important distinction between the permissibility of an action and what I call its meaning—the significance, for the agent and others, of the agent's willingness to perform that action for the reasons he or she does. Although permissibility does not, in general, depend on an agent's reasons for action, meaning obviously does, and many of the cases in which permissibility depends on an agent's reasons for action are cases in which permissibility depends on meaning.

In Chapter 3 I examine the ideas of treating a person as an end in him- or herself and treating a person as a mere means. Whether an action involves treating someone as an end or as a means depends on what the agent sees as reasons for treating that person one way or another. So if the injunction to treat humanity always as an end in itself and never merely as a means is a criterion of permissibility, there is an important class of cases in which the permissibility of an action depends on what the agent sees as reasons bearing on that action. I investigate this question first by considering the Kantian idea of treating rational nature as an end in itself, taking the idea of treating rational nature as a means to be identical with failing to treat it as an end. Bearing in mind the distinction, introduced in Chapter 1, between two kinds of moral judgment, I argue that this Kantian idea can be understood in either of two ways. It is very plausible to say that an action is permissible only if it is consistent with the idea of rational nature as an end in itself. Whether a given action satisfies this criterion, however, depends on the reasons for or against so acting, and not, in general, on what the agent takes those reasons to be. But the claim that, in a given action, an agent *treated* someone as an end, or failed to do so, can also be an observation about what the agent saw as reasons for acting one way rather than another. So understood, this is not a claim about the permissibility of the action but rather about its meaning.

Distinct from the Kantian ideas of treating someone as an end in him- or herself or merely as a means, there is a more specific idea of treating someone as a means, or "using" them, that applies only in cases in which some effect on a person is causally necessary to the achievement of the agent's aims. This idea is sometimes invoked, not as a characterization of wrongful action in general, but as an explanation for why actions of a certain type are wrong. The fact that an action involves using someone as a means in this more specific sense does sometimes make it fall within a broad class of wrongful action—actions that are wrong because they involve others in ways that have certain costs to them, without their consent. But this class of wrongs can be explained without reference to the idea of using someone, or of acting in a way that causally depends on someone as a means. I argue that these ideas are not in themselves of basic moral significance as determinants of permissibility. To say that in a certain action the agent was "just using" another person can, however, be an observation about the meaning of that action, and the fact that an action has this meaning can sometimes be relevant to its permissibility.

To say that an action is blameworthy is to make a claim about its meaning: to claim that the action indicates something about the agent's attitudes that impairs his or her relations with others. To blame someone, in my view, is to understand one's relations with that person as modified in the way that such a judgment holds to be appropriate. In Chapter 4 I elaborate and defend this interpretation of blame, explaining how it differs from and should be preferred to other interpretations that take blame to be a kind of negative assessment, a sanction, or the expression of some moral emotion, such as resentment. I examine the implications of this interpretation for the ethics of blame—for who may be blamed, who has standing to blame, and when one must blame. I also examine why blame might be thought to be appropriate only for actions that are undertaken freely, and explain why moral blame, as I understand it, does not presuppose free will.

In the course of this book I argue for a number of particular moral claims, including claims about which actions are permissible, about when intent matters to permissibility, and about various forms of moral responsibility. I hope that readers will be persuaded by what I have to say about these questions. But another important aim of the book is to identify and call attention to differences between the general moral notions in terms of which these particular judgments are expressed. These general notions are the dimensions of moral thinking referred to in the title: permissibility, meaning, and blame. My main claims are about how permissibility is to be understood; how it differs from meaning; how blameworthiness is a species of meaning; and how blame can be understood as a class of responses to this kind of meaning. I hope that readers who disagree with my particular moral claims will be led to reflect on the way that they understand these general moral notions. In particular, I hope they will consider whether the question of right and wrong as they understand it is what I am calling the question of permissibility. Similarly, I hope that those who disagree with me about blame will be inspired to make clear what they take moral blame to involve, and why blame as they understand it should be thought to require a particular kind of freedom.

1

The Illusory Appeal of Double Effect

How does the moral assessment of an action, in particular the moral permissibility of performing it, depend on the agent's intentions? This chapter and the next undertake an inquiry into this question. My main aim in this chapter is to explain why intent seems to be relevant to permissibility in the particular way claimed by the doctrine of double effect, even though this apparent significance is illusory. This leaves open the question, to be investigated in Chapter 2, of whether intent is relevant to permissibility in other ways. My second aim is to characterize the idea of moral permissibility and the ways in which it differs from other moral notions. I will begin with a few preliminary remarks about permissibility as I understand it.

Permissibility

The question of permissibility, "May one do X?" is generally asked as a precursor to a decision about whether to do X or not. So asked, it applies only to something that can be the object of an agent's decision, something that, if one were to decide to do it, would be done intentionally. But the question of permissibility, as I understand it, is broader than this. The question is not always a precursor to a decision but can also be asked retrospectively, or hypothetically, about the way a person behaved on some past, or imagined, occasion. One can ask, for example, whether it was permissible for a person to act in a way that posed a certain risk of harm to others, even if the person was unaware of that risk. The question of permissibility is always about something a person does or might do—a way he or she might govern him- or herself—and thus about something that *could* be the object of a possible decision. But it can be asked about a way of behaving characterized in a way that the agent was, at the time, unaware of, and hence about a way of behaving that was not intentional.

Any action can be characterized in indefinitely many ways. The phrase that replaces 'X' in the question of permissibility, "May one do X?" will be only a partial characterization, mentioning only a few of the properties that a proposed action would have, usually ones that are thought to raise a question about its permissibility. Thus, for example, I might ask, "May I give the patient this drug, given that it may well hasten his death?" The correct response may of course be "It depends," followed by a specification of additional facts about the action that are needed to determine its permissibility. Even this fuller specification will not uniquely identify an action. Various factors that characterize an action, such as the exact time and the exact way in which the agent will move her body, are often irrelevant to permissibility. What I wish to investigate is when and why the features of an action on which its permissibility depends will include facts about the agent's intentions in performing it.

Intent and Reasons

'Intention' is commonly used in a wider and a narrower sense.[1] When we say that a person did something intentionally, one thing we may mean is simply that it was something that he or she was aware of doing or realized would be a consequence of his or her action. This is the sense of 'intentionally' that is opposed to 'unintentionally': to say that you did something unintentionally is to claim that it was something you did not realize you were doing. But we also use 'intention' in a narrower sense. To ask a person what her intention was in doing a certain thing is to ask her what her aim was in doing it, and what plan guided her action—how she saw the action as promoting her objective.[2] To ask this is in part to ask what her reasons were for acting in such a way—which of the various features of what she realized she was doing were features she took to count in favor of acting in this way. This narrower sense of intention is at least very close to the sense of intention involved in the distinction, central to the doctrine of double effect, between the consequences of one's action that are intended (as ends or chosen means) and those that are merely foreseen.

One thing that these two senses of intention have in common is that each tells us something about an agent's view of the reasons bearing on his or her action. This is most obvious in the case of the narrower notion. Intention in the broader sense—the idea of what one does intentionally—is in the first instance a matter of what the agent understands herself to be doing rather than what her reasons were for doing it. But it is also true that if an agent does something intentionally in this broader sense—if she is aware of a certain aspect of her situation—then even if she does not take this aspect of what she is doing to provide a reason for her action, she at least does not (insofar as she is not acting irrationally) take it to constitute a sufficient reason not to act in that way. In either case, then, claims about what an agent does intentionally, or intends, have implications about her assessment of the reasons that bear on acting in that way.

Knowing an agent's intention in acting, and which things she is doing intentionally, can thus give us at least three kinds of information about the agent and her action. First, her intention, in the sense of her plan of action, tells us how she expects to move her body and to affect the world around her. Second, what it is that she is doing intentionally tells us what she believes about her situation and the likely effects of her action. Third, it also tells us something about how she evaluates these factors—which she sees as reasons for acting the way she plans to act, which as costs to be avoided if possible, which as costs to be borne, which as inconsequential.

The Apparent Significance of Intent

With this as background, let me turn to my main question, which is whether and how an agent's intention is relevant to the moral permissibility of what he or she does. This relevance may seem obvious. An agent's intention, it might be said, determines what the agent's action *is*—whether it is an instance of lying, for example, or murder—and what an action *is* in this sense must surely be relevant to its moral permissibility.

There is an important way in which this is quite true but not directly relevant to the question I am pursuing. An agent's aim in acting, her plan in acting, her beliefs about the likely effects of her action, and her evaluation of various features of her situation—which of them she sees as providing reasons, positive or negative, and which she sees as inconsequential—are, taken together, an important part of our basis for predicting the effects that her action will have. They are not, however, a complete basis for predicting those effects. An agent's understanding of her situation is often incomplete or mistaken, and the effects of a planned action may be quite different from what the agent expected. So, to assess an action we may need to draw on other information. But the agent's intention, and what she is doing intentionally, are a crucial starting point. Moreover, the agent's evaluation of various features of her situation tells us how her action is likely to be guided—which aspects of her situation she will attend to and how she is likely to respond if things do not go as she expects them to.

These factors are all clearly relevant to the permissibility of an agent's action, and later I will consider their significance in more detail. But this way in which intent can be relevant to the permissibility of an action is in an important sense derivative. What are of fundamental relevance in these cases are the effects of the agent's action on the world around her (or what it is reasonable to expect those effects to be). Her intention is relevant in the ways just described only because it tells us something about those effects. This is what I will call the *predictive* significance of intent. But the question I am interested in is whether an agent's intention is itself directly relevant to the permissibility of an action—whether, holding effects (or expected effects) constant, the permissibility of an action can depend on the agent's intention in performing it or, more generally, on what he or she saw as a reason for the action. So I will set aside for the moment the predictive significance of intent and concentrate on the question of how intent might be more directly relevant to permissibility.

Various lines of thought support the conclusion that intent is directly relevant to the moral assessment of an action. There is obviously an important moral difference between intentionally harming someone, causing harm negligently, and doing so through a freak accident. The difference between causing harm intentionally and doing so negligently, however, is not a difference in *permissibility*. Both are generally impermissible. The difference between them lies, rather, in the kind of fault that is involved when an agent acts impermissibly in these ways. The difference between causing harm in either of these ways and causing harm through a freak accident *does* appear to be a difference in permissibility. But what makes the difference here is not intent. What differentiates negligence from a freak accident is not the agent's aims, or necessarily what the agent believed about the likely effects of his or her action, but what he or she *should have believed,* under the circumstances, about the likely effects of that action.

It has seemed to many people that there are cases in which not just the overall moral assessment of an action but also its permissibility depends on the agent's intention. In wartime, for example, as I mentioned in the Introduction, it seems that there is an important moral difference between attacking a military target in a way that can be foreseen to lead to a certain number of civilian casualties and killing the same number of civilians in order to demoralize the population or discourage them from aiding the enemy. The difference between these two lines of action may seem to be one of intent. It may seem to lie in the fact that in the latter case, but not the former, those who carry out the attack intend to kill the civilians. They are not merely aware that this will be the effect of what they are doing; they are aiming at it, as a means to their end.

More generally, many people have been drawn to the doctrine of double effect, which holds that, although it can be permissible to do something that one can foresee will lead to the deaths of innocent people, when doing it is necessary to achieve some greater good, it is impermissible to kill the same number of innocent people as a means to achieving the same greater good. Although this doctrine is controversial, it is appealing because it seems to offer the best explanation of the distinction between terror bombing and tactical bombing, and also to explain other cases, such as the following.

> *Drug Shortage:* There are five people in Room B, and one person in Room A, all of whom have the same disease,

and all of whom will die if not treated soon. There is enough medicine on hand to cure all five of the people in Room B, but since the person in Room A has a more advanced case, it would take all of the available supply to save just him.

In this case it is clearly at least permissible to use all of the medicine to save the people in Room B. Now consider a different situation.

> *Transplant:* The five people in Room B are in need of organs—one needs a heart, two need a lung, and two need a kidney—and they will all die if they are not given transplants soon. Unfortunately, no organs are presently available. But there is a person in Room A, in for a checkup, who could be given a lethal injection instead of the inoculation he is expecting, thereby making his organs available to save the five others.

This is clearly impermissible. It might be tempting to explain the difference between these cases by saying that although it is permissible to let one die in order to save five, as in Drug Shortage, what is proposed in Transplant is to kill the one in order to save the five, and this is not permissible.

> *Drug/Transplant:* The people in Room B are the same as in Transplant, and the person in Room A is the same as in Drug Shortage. If the person in Room A dies of his illness, his organs will not be damaged and thus can be used to save the five. Is it permissible to withhold the drug from him?

Everyone with whom I have discussed these cases agrees that it is not. Why not? One answer would be that, as in Transplant, this would be a case of killing one to save five. But this cannot be the basic explanation. What is proposed in this case is the same as in Drug Shortage—to refrain from giving the person in Room A the available drug—and it was said in that first case that this would not be killing. If it is killing in this case, then this is because 'killing' is being used as a moral notion—that is to say, it is killing because it is wrong (for some other reason) rather than being wrong because it is killing. What, then, is this other reason?

The doctrine of double effect offers an explanation. Whereas in Drug Shortage the death of the one is merely a foreseeable consequence of giving the drug only to the five, in Drug/Transplant the death of the one is intended. What is proposed in that case is to withhold the drug from the one precisely in order to bring about the patient's death right away, so that his organs will be available for transplant in time to save the five. It is thus a case of intentionally killing an innocent person, which is absolutely impermissible according to the doctrine of double effect.

It might be suggested that the wrong involved in cases like Drug/Transplant is to be explained by rules that are peculiar to the hospital setting—rules specifying the duties that hospital personnel owe to patients—rather than by general moral principles. (Just as it might seem that the wrong involved in terror bombing is explained by the laws of war.) I will return to this possibility below, but it is worth noting here that what seem to be similar wrongs can occur in cases that do not involve hospitals or the obligations of doctors and nurses. Consider the following three cases.

> *Rescue I:* As I am driving home, I hear on my citizens-band radio that a car is stalled along a seldom-traveled road that I could easily take. The driver of the car is trying to deliver medicine to someone who will die unless he receives it within the next few hours. I could easily take that road and restart the stalled car.

Clearly I should do so.

> *Rescue II:* Same as the previous case, except I also hear that along another road I could take there is a stalled car that was taking medicine to five people in equally urgent need. There is not enough time for me to go to the aid of both cars.

Clearly in this case it is at least permissible for me to aid the second car, so as to save five rather than only one.

> *Rescue/Transplant:* Same as Rescue I, except that I know that there are five people in urgent need of transplants who will be saved if the patient awaiting the medicine dies very soon, as he will if I do not go to the aid of the stalled car.

It seems clearly impermissible to refrain from aiding the car in this case. As before, one plausible explanation is that in this case, but not in Rescue II, I would be intending that the one person should die, as a means to saving the five.

Like many others, I have found this explanation appealing. But there are well-known problems with it. First, to my knowledge no one has come up with a satisfying theoretical explanation of why the fact of intention, in the sense that is involved here—the difference between consequences that are intended and those that are merely foreseen—should make a moral difference. Second, there are cases in which applying this distinction seems to give the wrong answer. For example, in the well-known trolley-problem case it seems permissible to switch a runaway trolley onto a sidetrack on which it will hit only one person rather than allow it to continue straight ahead and hit five. But it also seems permissible to switch the trolley in the "Loop" case, proposed by Judith Thomson, in which the sidetrack loops around and rejoins the main line, so that if the trolley does not hit the one person and thereby come to a stop, it will continue around the loop and hit the five from the other side.[3] The answer in this case may be less clear than in the original one, but it is at least quite plausible to maintain that if it is permissible to turn the trolley onto the sidetrack in the first case, then it is permissible to do this in the second case as well.

These cases seem to differ in just the way I have described: in the second, but not the first, one switches the trolley only because it will, by hitting the one person, be prevented from hitting the five. This person's being hit by the trolley is intended as a means to the end of saving the others. Perhaps the distinction between harms that are intended and those that are merely foreseen, even though it makes a moral difference in the drug and transplant cases described above, does not make a difference in these cases. But this needs to be explained.[4]

Thomson also presents, as counterexamples to the kind of analysis we are considering, cases involving the use of lethal drugs for pain relief. Suppose that a patient is fatally ill and in great pain. The only course of medication that will relieve this pain will also cause the patient's death. Suppose that the patient wants to be given this drug. Does the permissibility of administering it depend on the doctor's intention in doing so—specifically, on whether the doctor intends to relieve the pain by causing the patient to die or intends to relieve the pain by giving the drug, which will, inevitably, also cause the patient's death? Thomson says, plausibly, that it does not.

This conclusion may draw support from the thought that it is not a bad thing, morally speaking, for a person in such circumstances to die sooner rather than later, and that therefore the usual moral strictures against causing death do not apply. But Thomson's objection retains its intuitive force in cases in which death is clearly a bad thing, such as military cases like the one I mentioned earlier. It is plausible to claim that it can be permissible in wartime to bomb a munitions factory even though this is certain to kill some civilians living nearby, but that it would not be permissible to kill the same number of civilians just as a way of undermining public support for the war, even if doing this would hasten the end of the conflict just as much as destroying the munitions plant would. These two actions clearly differ in moral permissibility. But is it equally clear that the moral difference between them is a matter of what is intended by the agents involved?

Thomson says that it is not. This would seem to be supported by thought experiments such as this: Suppose you were prime minister, and the commander of the air force described to you a planned air raid that would be expected to destroy a munitions plant and also kill a certain number of civilians, thereby probably undermining public support for the war. If he asked whether you thought this was morally permissible, you would not say, "Well, that depends on what your intentions would be in carrying it out. Would you be intending to kill the civilians, or would their deaths be merely an unintended but foreseeable (albeit beneficial) side effect of the destruction of the plant?"[5] Holding fixed the actual consequences of the raid and what the parties have reason to believe these consequences to be, might an action be permissible if performed by an agent with one intention but impermissible if performed by an agent with a different strategy in mind? I agree with Thomson in finding this implausible.

Explaining the Appeal of Double Effect

If this is implausible, why should the doctrine of double effect have seemed appealing as an explanation in the cases I considered earlier? Thomson suggests that the appeal of that doctrine depends on "a failure to take seriously enough the fact—I think it is plainly a fact—that the question whether it is morally permissible for a person to do a thing is just not the same as the question whether the person who does it is thereby shown to be a bad person."[6] As she says, a doctor who dislikes her patient and administers a lethal dose of pain killer, relishing the thought that this will be the last of him, is moved by morally objectionable reasons, even if an earlier death is in fact better for her patient. If she is moved by such reasons, then she is a morally bad person. But it does not follow that it is impermissible for her to administer the drug (or that the patient should have to wait until a different doctor, with better intentions, comes on duty).

There is something right in the suggestion that the appeal of the doctrine of double effect arises from a failure to distinguish clearly between assessing an agent and assessing the permissibility of her action. But in the form in which Thomson states it, this does not seem to explain the apparent significance of an agent's intention in cases of the kind we have been considering. Malicious thoughts of the kind just described, whether or not they operate as motives, certainly reflect badly on the character of the doctor. But no such thoughts have been involved in the cases we have been considering. The doctors in Transplant and Drug/Transplant are, we assume, moved purely by the desire to save as many lives as possible. The fact that they aim to do this by sacrificing an innocent person does not show them to be of bad character unless this is, independently, something that it is wrong to do. It therefore does not seem that we are tempted to think that it is wrong because it clearly indicates bad character and we fail to distinguish between the assessment of character and the question of permissibility.[7]

I believe that the truth in Thomson's point can be captured by putting it in a different way. The illusory appeal of intent as a way of explaining cases like Drug/Transplant flows, I suggest, from two facts about moral principles. The first is that although principles stating moral requirements specify that certain considerations normally count decisively for or against acting in a certain way, these principles almost always allow for exceptions. So, for example, according to the principle of fidelity to promises, the fact that one promised to do a certain thing is normally a conclusive reason for doing it—a reason that determines what one ought to do even if it would be more convenient or more advantageous to do something else. But there are exceptions. For example, one need not, and indeed should not, fulfill a promise to one person to do something fairly trivial if doing so would cause great harm to someone else. Fully understanding the morality of promising involves being able to recognize the considerations that do, and those that do not, justify such exceptions.

The second feature of moral principles that I have in mind is that they can be employed in either of two ways: as standards of criticism or as guides to deliberation. As guides to deliberation, moral principles answer a question of permissibility: "May one do X?" They also explain the answer by identifying the considerations that make it permissible or impermissible to do X under the circumstances in question. These considerations may concern what the agent sees as reasons for acting, or other features of his state of mind, but they need not and often do not do so. In what I will call their critical employment, however, a principle is used as the basis for assessing the way in which an agent went about deciding what to do on some real or imagined occasion. Used in this way, it provides the basis for answering a question of the form, "In deciding to do X under those circumstances, did Jones take the proper considerations into account and give them the right weight?" An answer to this question depends on an answer to the prior question, of which considerations are relevant to the permissibility of such an action and how they should be taken into account. But it goes beyond that question in asking whether the agent in question in fact took those considerations into account in the proper way.[8]

These two uses of moral principles are closely related, but there is a crucial difference between them. Criticism of the way an agent decided what to do is unavoidably predicated on assumptions about the agent's state of mind—in particular about what he or she took into account in deciding what to do and took as reasons for and against acting as he or she did. By contrast, when principles are used to guide deliberation, they do this merely by specifying which considerations do, and which do not, count for or against various courses of action. I will refer to these applications of principles as their *critical* and their *deliberative* uses.[9]

It is easy to overlook this distinction. Since principles tell agents which considerations count for or against an action, it is natural to say that agents follow these principles when they take these considerations as reasons, and that when they do not, their failure to do so makes their actions wrong. But what makes an action wrong is the consideration or considerations that count decisively against it, not the agent's failure to give these considerations the proper weight.

Suppose, for example, that I have promised to sell you my house, and that under the circumstances this counts as a decisive reason for doing so. In particular, the fact that I could get more money by breaking my promise and selling the house to someone else is not a sufficient reason to do that. But suppose I do break the promise in order to get this benefit. In describing what was defective about my action, you might say that I acted wrongly in taking my own advantage as sufficient reason to break my promise. This would be true, as a critical observation about the decision I made. At a more fundamental level, however, what *made* my action wrong was not the fact that I acted for a bad (selfish) reason, but rather the fact that I had promised to sell you the house. Given that there were no countervailing considerations that would justify an exception to the requirement that promises be kept, this fact counted decisively against my selling the house to someone else.

The distinction is even clearer when we view the case prospectively. Suppose I ask, while deciding what to do, "Must I do what I promised? Why shouldn't I sell to the other person, since it would be more profitable?" You would not reply, "That would be wrong, because you would be aiming at your own benefit (or acting for the sake of your benefit)." It is true that I would be open to criticism for taking my own advantage to be sufficient reason for breaking a promise. But this is criticism of the way I went about deciding, not an explanation of why my action would be wrong. What makes it wrong for me to sell to the second potential buyer is that I promised to sell to the first one.

Supporters of the doctrine of double effect may disagree, or at least seem to disagree, because they take the relevant category of moral criticism to be that of a good action. Since an agent's intention in acting is crucial in making what he does an action, and making that action the type of action it is, they might argue, this intention is crucial in determining whether it is a good action.[10] Since they believe that an agent, in deciding what to do, should be guided by whether a proposed action is good, it might seem that they are proposing an alternative answer to the question of permissibility, and disagreeing with me about the relevance of intent in answering this question. What I am saying, however, is that intent seems relevant to permissibility only if one does not distinguish what I am calling the deliberative and critical uses of a principle. And indeed, the idea of a good action is naturally understood as falling on the critical side of my distinction. This raises the interesting question of whether those who disagree about double effect are disagreeing about the application of a single moral concept—about what makes certain actions impermissible—or whether they are employing different categories of moral appraisal—one side talking about permissibility, the other about the goodness of actions. If they are employing different categories, this leads to the further question of what reasons there are for taking one or the other of these categories as the one that is important for certain purposes—for example, as having the fundamental role in deliberation.

I believe that the two features of moral principles that I have described provide the best explanation of our reactions to Transplant and to the other examples I have discussed above. First, although the examples differ in many ways, they all have the same structure: they concern general principles that sometimes admit of exceptions, and they raise questions about when those exceptions apply. For example, it is normally impermissible to act in ways that can be foreseen to cause serious harm. The runaway trolley case shows that this principle has exceptions: it is sometimes permissible to act in ways that can be foreseen to cause serious harm to some people if this is the only way to prevent similar harm to a greater number. Transplant shows that although the possibility of saving others sometimes justifies an exception to the prohibition against causing foreseeable harm, it does not always do so. Similarly, Drug Shortage and Rescue II show that there are exceptions to the principle requiring us to aid others when we can: in these cases it is permissible to fail to save some because this is the only way to save others. But our reactions to Drug/Transplant and Rescue/Transplant reflect our judgment that the possibility of saving others does not always justify an exception to this principle.

The underlying question raised by these cases is why the principles involved in them should have this particular form: why a consideration that justifies an exception to a principle in some cases should not do so in others. I will return to this question below. What I want to point out here is that if these cases have the structure I have just described, then the second feature of moral principles that I discussed above—the distinction between the critical and deliberative uses of a principle, and the ease of overlooking this distinction—can explain why it is tempting, but nonetheless mistaken, to think that they are cases in which the intentions of the agent play a fundamental role in determining permissibility.

It is tempting to say that what would make it wrong for an agent to fail to save the person in Drug/Transplant or in Rescue/Transplant is the fact that she would be intending that person's death—that is to say, she would be taking the advantages of his dying sooner as sufficient reason not to save him. It would be quite correct to say this if we were taking the relevant principle in its *critical* employment and assessing the way in which the agent decided what to do. That is, it would be quite correct to say that her way of making this decision was defective because she *took* a certain consideration (the possibility of saving five others) as justifying an exception to the principle requiring one to aid others, when in fact that consideration did not justify an exception to the principle in this case.

But the question of permissibility is answered by considering the relevant principles in their *deliberative* employment. What makes a proposed action wrong is the consideration that the relevant principle identifies as counting decisively against it (given the absence of relevant countervailing considerations). In the promise-keeping example discussed above, this was the fact that I had promised to sell you my house. In Drug/ Transplant and Rescue/Transplant, it is the fact that there is a person who is in need of aid that the agent can easily provide. A person who takes the possibility of saving others via transplant as justifying an exception to the duty to aid in these cases, or takes the possibility of selling his house for a higher price as justifying an exception to the obligation to keep a promise, makes a mistake in so doing. What makes this a mistake, and what makes the corresponding actions impermissible, are the considerations that support the relevant obligations.

The distinction in question here—between the deliberative use of a principle to decide whether a certain action is permissible and its critical use to assess an agent's process of decision making—is similar to the distinction mentioned by Thomson, between assessing an action and assessing an agent. But the distinction I am calling attention to is narrower and, for that reason, easier to overlook. It is the distinction between the permissibility of an action and a special kind of agent assessment, in which what is being assessed is not the agent's overall character but rather the quality of the particular piece of decision making that led to the action in question.

Military Cases

The same analysis also explains why it is tempting, albeit mistaken, to appeal to intent to distinguish between impermissible "terror bombing" and "tactical bombing," which is seen as permissible. Discussion of these cases is shaped by assumptions about the relevant principles applicable to the conduct of war. It is often assumed that these principles are formulated in terms of what agents may *intend.* But this is not the only or, I believe, the best way to understand them. The principle relevant to these cases states a class of exceptions to the general prohibition against the use of deadly force, and specifies the limits of those exceptions. It can be seen as having something like the following form.[11]

> In war, one is sometimes permitted to use destructive and potentially deadly force of a kind that would normally be prohibited. But such force is permitted only when its use can be expected to bring some military advantage, such as destroying enemy combatants or warmaking materials, and it is permitted only if expected harm to noncombatants is as small as possible, compatible with gaining the relevant military advantage, and only if this harm is "proportional" to the importance of this advantage.

> In the example of tactical bombing that Thomson discusses, it is assumed that the destruction of the munitions

plant constitutes a military advantage in the relevant sense. Bombing it is therefore permissible if (and only if) the conditions I have listed are fulfilled: only if harm to noncombatants is minimized and the expected harm is "proportional."

If there is no munitions plant, but a bombing raid that would kill the same number of noncombatants would hasten the end of the war by undermining morale, this raid (a pure case of "terror bombing") would be not permissible under the rationale just given. It is impermissible because it can be expected to kill people, and the circumstances do not provide a justification for doing this under the principle just stated. The death of noncombatants is not rendered a "military advantage" by the fact that it would shorten the war by undermining public morale. So the fact that it would do this does not bring the case under the exception, just described, to the prohibition against doing what can be reasonably foreseen to cause loss of life.

It remains true, in my view, that a person who intends to kill noncombatants in order to shorten the war by undermining morale (and has no further justification for her action) acts wrongly—she has an intention that she should abandon. But this truth should not be taken to suggest that intention has a fundamental role in determining the impermissibility of this action, in the way claimed by the doctrine of double effect. The intention is wrongful because the act intended is wrongful, and the act is wrongful because of its likely consequences, not (fundamentally) because of the intention.

Two lines of thought might lead to the conclusion that in cases of the kind we are discussing, the permissibility of an action depends on the agents' intentions. The first of these is the one that I have been arguing is mistaken; the second, which turns on the predictive significance of intent, is valid but does not give intention a fundamental role.

The first line of thought moves from the true premise that what is morally faulty about the reasoning of those who think that terror bombing is permissible lies in the fact that they take shortening the war by demoralizing the public as a consideration that justifies the bombing. It then moves to the false conclusion that this fact about their reasoning is also what makes their action wrong. This move fails to distinguish between the critical employment of a principle and its deliberative employment.

To understand the second line of thought leading to the conclusion that intent can be relevant to permissibility, it is helpful to notice that there is something artificial about the way I have presented these examples. I have been assuming that the consequences of an action (in these cases, the consequences of a bombing raid) can be predicted on grounds that are independent of the intentions of the agents who carry it out. It is of course true that two actions done with different intent, such as a raid carried out by a pilot who wants to minimize civilian casualties and one carried out by a pilot who relishes them, can have exactly the same consequences. But this is not what we normally have reason to expect.

To see the importance of this difference, consider a more artificial case, in which consequences are certain to be independent of intent. Suppose that the raid in question is to be carried out not by piloted planes, but by missiles, which are preprogrammed to seek out certain targets and avoid others. So we can assume that the consequences of firing the missiles—the effects on the military target and on civilians in the surrounding area—can be predicted with considerable accuracy, and in any event do not depend on the way anyone involved in carrying out the attack responds after the missiles are launched. Suppose that the question the commander asks you, as prime minister, is whether, given these consequences, it is permissible for him to launch the missile. In this case it seems clear that your answer should depend on whether, given the likely consequences of the strike, there is a justification for it that meets the relevant criteria. You should not say, "Well, it depends on your intentions in launching it. When you push the button to launch the missile, will you be doing this in order to destroy the factory or in order to undermine morale by killing the civilians?" Here Thomson's criticism seems to me entirely correct.

But in the world as we know it, things are not like this. If the planes dropping bombs are guided by human beings, then the effects of the raid will depend on how the agents carrying it out respond to the changing circumstances that they are presented with. We could, of course, assume that the pilots, whatever their personal valuations of the alternatives may be, will strictly follow prescribed orders and procedures. If this is so, then the case will be like that of the automated missile, and the intentions of the agents will not be relevant to the permissibility of the raid. But if it is not so, if the way the agents react, and how hard they try to avoid harm to noncombatants, depends on whether they intend to avoid such harm if they possibly can, then their intentions—what they see as reasons—will matter to the permissibility of the raid. In such a case it will be quite appropriate for the prime minister to ask about the intentions of those who will carry out the raid. Their intentions will not have the kind of significance attributed to them by the doctrine of double effect, but they will have predictive significance, which, although it is derivative, is by no means unimportant.

My discussion of these cases has presupposed certain principles about the conduct of war. I have not offered any defense of these principles or an explanation of their moral status. In particular, I have not offered any explanation or justification for the importance they attach to the distinction between combatants and noncombatants. My point has been merely that these principles need not be understood as making permissibility depend on intent. Those who believe that there is an important moral difference between tactical bombing and terror bombing need to defend some version of the combatant/noncombatant distinction. But they need not be saddled with the additional burden of defending the relevance of intent, or the doctrine of double effect.

Transplant Cases Reconsidered

Returning now to the hospital and rescue cases, it is important here as well to be clear, first, about how the principles that are guiding the discussion should be understood and, second, about whether these principles are being applied in a deliberative or in a critical way. The most obvious principles at work in these cases are the one (in Transplant) specifying a duty not to kill and the one (in Drug/Transplant and Rescue/Transplant) specifying a duty to aid when one can (in the case of Drug/Transplant, perhaps also the special duty on the part of hospital workers to aid those in their care). The question is what exceptions there are to these principles. In particular, when does the possibility of saving others give rise to an exception?

The discussion of these cases also presupposes that it is impermissible simply to take a living person's organs, even if this would benefit others, but that once a person is dead, his or her organs are available for use to save others. Like the distinction between combatants and noncombatants, this principle might be questioned, but it is presupposed in the examples as I have presented them. It is this principle that explains why it is necessary to bring about the patient's death (by giving him or her the wrong injection, in Transplant, or by withholding medication, in Drug/Transplant) in order for the organs to become available. This is what forces on us the question of whether the possibility of saving others justifies an exception to the underlying principles against killing or requiring saving.

Once the question is posed in this way, however, the idea that there are such exceptions becomes bizarre. The general form of the question is this: so long as this person is alive, we have an obligation to him to do X. If we were freed from this obligation, we could do something good. Does this count as a justification to kill the person, or to fail to save him? The answer is clearly that it does not. Perhaps a justifiable form of the obligation in question would incorporate an exception for cases in which good of the relevant kind could be achieved by abrogating it. (In the case at hand, this exception would allow us to take the organs of a living person when they could be used to save the lives of a greater number.) Assuming that the obligation does not incorporate such an exception, the idea that this should lead to justification for bringing about the person's death is absurd.

This absurdity does not itself depend on the idea that an individual has a special claim to his or her organs, although that is the particular moral claim that is at issue in the case we are discussing. The same absurdity could arise with respect to any underlying moral claim. Consider, for example, the question of how life-saving equipment, such as heart-lung machines, should be allocated. Suppose we say that when there is a shortage of such equipment, it should be allocated in such a way as to save the most lives. Then the question arises whether, if a machine is allocated to one patient on this basis, it may be taken away and given to another patient if this would lead to the saving of more lives. (Perhaps the other patient would need it for less time, so it could then be passed on to a third.) Suppose the answer to this question is that this is not permissible: once a person is put on such a machine, he or she cannot be taken off of it so long as he or she is alive and needs the machine to stay alive. Assuming this to be the case, suppose that a person who is being kept alive by a heart-lung machine develops an infection that could be easily treated but will be fatal if not treated. (I am assuming that this person has good prospects of recovering and being taken off the machine eventually, but that this will take time.) Does the fact that we could save more lives by transferring the machine to someone who will need it less long release us from the obligation to treat this patient's infection? The suggestion that it does is what I am saying is absurd. This is not to say that the assumptions that lead to this suggestion—about how scarce equipment should be allocated and whether, once allocated, it can be taken away—may not be mistaken. The point is just that once they are accepted, the last suggestion becomes absurd.

Like the original transplant cases, the example I have just given involves medical treatment. But the point I am making is not restricted to such cases. To state it in general terms, if we have some obligation to a person so long as he is alive, the advantages of our being relieved of this obligation by his dying do not justify an exception to the principle requiring us not to kill that person, or to save that person's life when we can easily do so. This point applies to Rescue/Transplant as well as to Drug/Transplant. In both cases, the proposed course of action is impermissible for the reason just mentioned: they are cases in which we have a duty to save the person, and the advantages of being released from the obligation not to take his organs do not justify an exception to this duty.

In this respect, the rationale for the proposed courses of action in these cases is quite different from that in Drug Shortage, and Rescue II. In those cases it is claimed that an agent is released from a duty to save one person by the possibility of saving a greater number. But there is no appeal to the idea that the death of the one person makes this possible by releasing the agent from a duty that he or she has to that person so long as he or she is alive.

What makes the proposed courses of action in Drug/Transplant and Rescue/Transplant wrong (and differentiates these cases from Drug Shortage and Rescue II) is therefore not the agents' intent. It is true that an agent in Drug/Transplant or Rescue/Transplant who accepted the proposed rationale for a course of action would be mistakenly taking the fact that the death of the one patient would release us from an obligation as a reason to save him or her. But to say this is to make the shift I have been calling attention to, from the deliberative application of the relevant principles (which is relevant to the question of permissibility) to a critical application of these principles (an assessment of the way the agent went about deciding what to do).

The account I am proposing also differs from one based on the doctrine of double effect in a further way, which should be noted. According to an account of the latter kind, there is a deep similarity between the courses of action involved in Transplant, Drug/Transplant, Rescue/Transplant, and terror bombing. What is done in all of these cases is wrong because it involves intending to bring about the death of innocent people as a means to some greater good. According to my account there is a more abstract similarity between these cases. In each one, an agent who follows a certain course of action would mistakenly take a certain factor as justifying an exception to a principle ruling out killing, or requiring one to give aid. But what makes the proposed actions wrong depends on the applicable principles and the explanation of why the proposed exceptions are not genuine. At this more substantive level, the cases are very different. To understand them we need to examine the different principles that are at work, and the case for possible exceptions to them, rather than appeal to a general prohibition against aiming at the death of an innocent person.

2

The Significance of Intent

I argued in Chapter 1 that an agent's intentions are not relevant to permissibility of an action in the particular way that the doctrine of double effect would claim. I allowed that an agent's intentions are relevant to forms of moral assessment other than questions of permissibility, and I tried to show that the plausibility of the doctrine of double effect arises from a failure to distinguish between different forms of moral assessment and different ways in which a moral principle may be employed.

This distinction is frequently overlooked. In explaining why certain actions are impermissible, people often refer to intent—to an agent's reasons for acting—when in fact what makes these actions wrong is the considerations that count against it, not the agent's view of those considerations. I did this myself, for example, in stating the following principle.

Principle M: In the absence of special justification, it is
not permissible for one person, A, in order to get
another person, B, to do some act, X (which A wants B
to do and which B is morally free to do or not do but
would otherwise not do), to lead B to expect that if he or
she does X then A will do Y (which B wants but believes
that A will otherwise not do), when in fact A has no
intention of doing Y if B does X, and A can reasonably
foresee that B will suffer significant loss if he or she does
X and A does not reciprocate by doing Y.[1]

This principle rules out a certain kind of manipulation,
which it describes as intentionally misleading someone about
one's own intentions in order to get him or her to act a certain
way. If, as Principle M says, A misleads B about what he intends to do "in order to" get B to do something that he would
otherwise not do, then A is misleading B intentionally in both
of the senses of 'intentionally' that I mentioned at the beginning of Chapter 1: A is aware that his action will have this effect and he counts this in favor of acting in the way that he
does. But the impermissibility of what A is doing does not depend on the fact that A is acting intentionally in either of these
senses.

Suppose that A's main purpose in acting was to achieve
some other aim, and B's being misled was just a foreseen side
effect of his action. If being misled in this way involves serious
costs for B, then (absent some special justification) A is acting
impermissibly in failing to protect B against this cost. Further,
even if A is unaware that what he is doing will lead to B's being

misled and suffering a serious loss as a result, if he *should* be aware of this given the information available to him, then he is still acting impermissibly even though he is not misleading B intentionally in either of the two senses mentioned.[2]

Principle M characterizes a certain kind of wrong. An action would not be wrong *in that way* if it did not involve intentionally misleading someone. But it would not follow that what the agent would then be doing was permissible. The other features of the action described in Principle M might still make it wrong. So, although the idea of acting intentionally plays a role in characterizing a particular form of morally objectionable action, it does not in this case play a role in drawing the line between what is permissible and what is impermissible.

It might be objected that an agent's intention in both of the senses just mentioned is crucial to identifying what it is that he does, and that A would be performing a different type of action in each of the three situations I have imagined. This is quite correct. But what is at issue is not whether the agent's intent can determine the type of action he or she performs. (Obviously, it can.) The question is whether the agent's intent is crucial to the permissibility of his or her action.

Expression and Expectation Cases

It is not difficult to think of cases in which the permissibility of an action depends on the agent's reasons for so acting, albeit in a less fundamental way than the doctrine of double effect would suggest. Some actions involve presenting oneself as being moved by certain reasons. (I will call cases of this kind *ex-*

pression cases.) In inquiring about the health of a sick relative, for example, I may present myself as being moved by affectionate concern for that person's welfare. Suppose, however, that I am not moved by this reason at all. I might telephone the relative and inquire about her health just to get my mother to stop nagging me, or to curry favor with my wealthy grandfather. This may not make it impermissible for me to call. Perhaps a call from me would do so much to cheer the person up that I should call, despite the fact that it would be hypocritical. But the fact that I would not be calling for the reason that I would be representing myself as being moved by is a consideration that at least counts against the action, and could do so decisively in the absence of other considerations to the contrary.

Something similar is true in a wider range of what might be called *expectation* cases. These are cases in which someone enters into a certain relation with an agent—a conversation, perhaps, or some form of cooperation—only because he or she assumes (perhaps without the agent's having done anything to encourage this assumption) that the agent has certain intentions, or is moved by certain reasons and not others. In these cases, facts about an agent's intentions, or about the reasons he or she is moved by, are relevant to the permissibility of the agent's action. But they are again relevant only in a derivative way, as a consequence of a more basic moral requirement not to mislead others or take advantage of their mistaken beliefs about one's intentions. So the question remains whether there are cases in which facts about an agent's reasons for acting are relevant to permissibility in a more fundamental way.

Attempts, Mistakes of Fact, and Larger Courses of Action

One way in which an agent's intention can appear to make an otherwise unobjectionable action impermissible is by making it part of a larger course of action that is impermissible. Suppose, for example, a man is buying rat poison. If he were buying the poison to stop the rats in his cellar from destroying the grain his family needs to survive the winter, then this would be permissible. But things seem different if he is buying it in order to kill his wife. The permissibility of his buying the poison thus seems to depend on his intention in doing so.

It is certainly impermissible for the man to put rat poison in his wife's food. What makes this impermissible is not his intent, but the fact that putting the poison in her food can be expected to cause her death. Given that he has every reason to believe that it would have this effect, he should not put poison in her food, and if he has the intention of doing this, he should abandon his intention. So one thing we can say about a person who is buying poison with the intention of using it to kill his wife is that what he intends to do is impermissible, and that he should abandon this intention.

But what should we say about the act of buying the rat poison itself? Is *it* rendered impermissible by the fact that the agent intends, at the time, to use the poison to kill his wife? One thing the larger intention does is to supply the reason for buying the poison. So we might say that buying the rat poison is wrong because of the reason for which he does it. But the larger intention also affects the action in a different way. Suppose that when the man bought the poison, he himself did not intend to kill anyone, but he had good reason to believe that his neighbor, who had asked him to buy it, was intending to use it to carry out a murder. In this case, buying the poison for the neighbor would be impermissible because in buying it he would be facilitating a murder. For this to be so, the man need not *intend* (in the narrower sense) to be aiding in his neighbor's plan. He need not count the fact that it will help the neighbor bring about a murder as one of his reasons for buying the poison. In order for it to be impermissible for him to buy the poison for the neighbor, it is enough that he reasonably believes that in doing so he would be aiding such a plan, or that he should believe this, given the information available to him.

Now return to the original case in which the man is buying poison in order to carry out a murder himself. A person who intends to do something believes that he will do it, or at least that he will try and that he will have a reasonable chance of success. So, just as in the previous case, in buying the poison the man is facilitating a murder, in this case one that he has reason to believe that he himself will carry out. This seems to me the most plausible explanation of how intention is relevant to permissibility in the case of actions that are part of larger plans. In particular, it is more accurate to say that such actions are impermissible because they facilitate other wrongs than to say simply that they are impermissible because they are done for certain reasons. These two ways of explaining the impermissibility are closely related: the larger plan provides a reason for the smaller action *because* it facilitates that action. Nonetheless, the two explanations are distinguishable, and facilitation provides a better explanation of what makes these acts wrong. They are wrong not because of the reason for which *they* are done, but because the agent's larger intention changes their likely consequences. This is an instance of what I called in Chapter 1 the *predictive* significance of intent.

This appeal to facilitation may seem forced. It may seem that there is a stronger reason to say that buying the poison is impermissible when the person's own intention is to use it to kill someone than there is in the case in which he is merely facilitating the action of someone else. But is this difference a matter of the permissibility of the agent's buying the poison? It is true in the one-person version of the example that at the time the agent buys the poison, he has an intention that he should abandon. So he is, at that time, open to moral criticism for something that goes beyond facilitation.

This further criticism is related to the wrongfulness of facilitation in a way that brings out a difference between the one-person and two-person examples. To see this, consider other actions, more innocent in themselves than buying poison, which may also facilitate the planned murder. Suppose that, to carry out his plan to poison his wife, the man has to get up very early in the morning, before his wife is awake. In doing this, as well, he facilitates murder. Should we conclude that it is impermissible for him to get up early? The implausibility of this suggestion can be explained in the following way. In the case of the man who was buying poison for his neighbor, it is impermissible for him to buy it only if not buying it is the only way he can avoid facilitating a murder. If he could buy it but avoid giving it to the neighbor, or prevent the neighbor from using it, then buying it would be permissible. In the case of the man who is buying the poison for a murder that he himself intends to get up early in the morning to carry out, not buying the poison (or not getting up early) is clearly not the only way for him to avoid facilitating murder. He could instead abandon his murderous plan, and as I have said, this is something he should do. This is what makes it implausible to say that it is impermissible for him to get up early. What he ought to do is to abandon his murderous plan. Whether he gets up or stays in bed is, in itself, immaterial.[3]

This analysis can also explain the apparent significance of intent in a wider range of cases. In the debates about the permissibility of creating human embryos by cloning, for example, it is common to distinguish between what is called "reproductive" cloning, in which embryos are produced for the purpose of creating a new human being, and "therapeutic" cloning, in which embryos are created for the purpose of producing, or discovering how to produce, material to be used in medical treatment. It is widely held that the former is impermissible while the latter is not, and thus, it would seem, that the permissibility of these procedures depends on the intentions of those who undertake them.

The apparent significance of intent in this case can be explained in the ways I have just suggested. Assume, for purposes of argument, that it would be wrong to create a human infant who could reasonably be expected to be an exact genetic replica of a previously existing person. (I leave aside the question of why and in what way this would be wrong.) It would follow that it would be wrong to create an embryo by cloning with the intention of producing a genetic replica of a previously existing person, because in creating such an embryo one would be facilitating an action that would be wrong.

The difference between reproductive cloning and therapeutic cloning might be understood in a different way, however. Suppose there is a significant, but rebuttable, moral objection to creating a human embryo by cloning (perhaps because this involves interfering with or manipulating the reproductive process in an objectionable way). This objection might be outweighed in some cases. In particular, it might be outweighed by the fact that the cells produced would be used to save a life. This would explain why therapeutic cloning is permissible. But in a case in which one's aim in creating an embryo is simply to create a new human being, there is no reason to expect that any life-saving benefit will result. So the objection to cloning stands unrebutted. This is an instance of what I have called the predictive significance of intent, but with a slightly different twist. In this case the intent to produce a new human being affects the permissibility of reproductive cloning not by making an objectionable result likely but by showing that a certain valuable result is not likely to occur, and therefore cannot be cited as a justification for creating the embryo.

Thus far I have been considering cases in which the significance of intent is explained by its predictive role. In searching for cases in which intent might have a more fundamental role in determining permissibility, it is natural to look to cases in which the larger intended effect of an action does not in fact occur, and perhaps was never even likely to occur. One class of cases in which this is so is the class of attempts—cases in which agents set out to do something impermissible but fail to bring about the harmful results that they intend. If such an attempt is unsuccessful, then—it may seem—there is no actual harmful effect to render the action wrong. It is therefore tempting to say that what makes the action wrong is just that the effect was intended—that, for example, the agent was acting with the aim of killing an innocent person.

From the point of view of a deliberating agent, there is little difference between deciding to kill a person and deciding to attempt to kill him. In either case, the action is one that the agent must believe to have at least a significant probability of resulting in the person's death. Given this belief, the action is one that (in the absence of special justification) the agent should see as wrong. But it is important here to distinguish clearly between the considerations that make an action wrong and factors that make it an action that the agent should *see* as wrong.[4]

This distinction is clearest in cases in which the action an agent proposes to take is in fact utterly harmless. A person who believes in voodoo, for example, may think that by sticking pins in a doll he is bringing about the agonizing death of his former girlfriend's new lover. But there is no reason to think that sticking pins into a doll is in fact harmful. So how could it be impermissible? There does seem to be *something* wrong with the action I have described. What is wrong with it, however, is not that it is impermissible but rather that the agent should (given his beliefs) *see it as* impermissible. And what the agent should see as counting against the action is the fact that (as he sees things) it will cause the death of an innocent person, not the fact that in performing this action he would be acting with the intention of bringing this about.

Permissibility and the Objective 'Ought'

I mentioned earlier, in discussing negligence, that what an agent knew, or should have known, can make a difference in the permissibility of what she has done. Judith Thomson, however, denies that this is so. She believes that 'ought' should be understood in an "objective" manner, which she illustrates with the following example.

> *Day's End:* B always comes home at 9:00 P.M., and the first thing he does is to flip the light switch in his hallway. He did so this evening. B's flipping the switch caused a circuit to close. By virtue of an extraordinary series of coincidences, unpredictable in advance by anybody, the circuit's being closed caused a release of electricity (a small lightning flash) in A's house next door. Unluckily, A was in its path and was therefore badly burned.[5]

Thomson says that in this example B has "infringed a claim of A's." One might be inclined to disagree, on the grounds that B, assuming he has no reason to think that this "extraordinary series of coincidences" will occur, is at not fault or open to moral criticism for flipping the switch. But Thomson rejects the idea that an agent violates someone's claim only if he is at fault in behaving as he did. The core of the idea of a claim, she argues, is that actions violating it are ones that an agent ought not to do, where 'ought' is understood in the objective sense that does not entail fault. This is the sense in which we might say, for example, that if giving a baby aspirin made his condition worse, then we ought not to have given the baby aspirin, even though there was at the time every indication that it would make him better. Using 'ought' in this sense, Thomson says that B ought not to have flipped the switch, given that it would cause A serious harm. In support of this thesis she says the following about Day's End. "Wouldn't it be weird in us, knowing what will happen if B flips the switch, to say, 'Look B, we know something you don't know. If we tell you, then it will be true to say that you ought not flip the switch, but not if we don't tell you.' The weirdness of that performance is a sign that 'ought' is at least typically used objectively."[6]

I do not think that what B does in Day's End is impermissible. One ought not do what one sees, or should see, will cause serious harm to someone. One ought to take due care not to cause harm. But this requirement is not violated in Day's End if it was only "by virtue of an extraordinary series of coincidences, unpredictable in advance by anybody," that what B did led to A's being harmed. If it is true that B ought not to have flipped the switch, this is true only in a sense of 'ought not' that seems to me to lack the moral content that the idea of permissibility has. Both A and B may wish, after the fact, that B had not flipped the switch, but in doing so B did not act impermissibly.

This conclusion might be supported by saying that the point of view expressed in the objective sense of 'ought' that Thomson describes involves a kind of omniscience that prevents it from being identified with the point of view of a deliberating agent, and therefore prevents it from capturing the idea of permissibility that is appropriate to the latter outlook. But it could also be claimed that exactly the reverse is the case. As Thomson might point out, if B were to learn later of the harmful consequence of his action, he would rightly regard this as a consideration that counted strongly against so acting. Of course, B was not at fault for acting in this way, given that no one could have known his action would have the result it did. But this notion of fault, it might be said, is a matter of assessment of the way B decided what to do, and thus is exactly the kind of thing I have been distinguishing from the kind of question that permissibility involves. What is relevant for the purposes of answering this action-guiding question, it might be said, is the actual result of the action, not what the agent knows about that result. Therefore, it might be concluded, when permissibility is clearly distinguished from critical assessment of an agent's decision making (and hence from fault) it turns out to coincide with what an agent ought to do in the objective sense.

This response turns on a confusion about the relation between fault and permissibility. Both permissibility and fault are determined by the principles that we can ask each other to use in deciding what to do. Permissibility, as I have said, is determined by the use of these principles in guiding deliberation: an act is permissible if, under the circumstances, it would be licensed by these principles. The same principles, used critically, determine fault. Because the same principles are involved in both uses, permissibility, unlike the objective 'ought,' is a notion that normally entails fault. If what I did was impermissible, then there were considerations that counted decisively against it and, hence, at least in most cases, I was in some way at fault in failing to take those considerations properly into account and in performing the action despite them.[7]

But even though impermissibility normally entails fault,

assessments of fault go beyond assessments of permissibility, and take into account facts about motivation, such as whether the agent was acting out of malice, and facts about what the agent believed, whether or not those beliefs were reasonable.[8] In deciding whether an action would be permissible, however, we must attend to more objective factors. Permissibility is determined by those features of our situation that we should take as counting for or against an action.

This is what makes it seem that the idea of permissibility might coincide with the objective 'ought.' To see why it does not, we need to consider what principles we have reason to accept as guiding agents in deciding what to do. In deciding whether to accept a principle, we are of course centrally concerned with the way in which the actions it would allow would affect us. It would, for example, be reasonable for us to reject a principle that did not require others to take the fact that an action would cause us serious harm as a strong, indeed normally conclusive, reason against that action.

This principle is fundamental, but other considerations, flowing from the fact that we are commonly dealing with imperfect information, are also relevant. If any principle that it would not be reasonable to reject would require us to take C as a consideration counting strongly against an action, then, since it may not be immediately obvious whether C obtains or not, in considering any other principles it would not be reasonable to reject, we are required to be on the lookout for C, and to take reasonable steps to find out whether or not it obtains. What makes it permissible to act in a certain way is not the fact that, having done these things, we *believe* that so acting poses no danger to others; rather, it is the fact about the world that taking these steps puts us in a position to see: that the available evidence does not indicate that our action poses such a danger.

Given this account of what is required of us, we can explain the "weirdness" of the remark that Thomson imagines being made to B in Day's End. First, given that the imagined interlocutor (call her C) knows that flipping the switch will cause A serious injury, it is odd for her to say that if she told B what she knows, then it would be true that B ought not flip the switch, but that this would not be true if she did not tell him. C's remark is odd because it seems to suggest that it would be B's knowing about the harm, rather than the harm itself, that would make it the case that he ought not flip the light switch. If B knows about the harm, then he should count *it* as a reason against turning on the light. But it is still true that his knowing about it makes an important moral difference. In the original example, the injury to A was said to be due to "an extraordinary series of coincidences, unpredictable in advance by anybody." In the modified example, C knows about this effect and could easily tell B. So the situation is quite different. But the fact that knowledge makes this difference is quite consistent with the fact that, in a situation in which B has this knowledge, it is still the fact that is known, not the fact of his knowing it, that he is to take as counting against his action.

The question of permissibility is a question that can be asked by a deliberating agent, and one that a normal agent can be expected to be able to answer. The answer to this question is not just a matter of what is in fact the case (whether anyone could know it or not). But at the same time, permissibility is not merely a matter of what a particular agent believes the facts to be. It depends also on what it is reasonable for the agent to believe in the situation, what it is reasonable for the agent to do to check those beliefs, and whether the agent has done those things.[9] If, in the original version of Day's End, B has satisfied these requirements, and in fact there is no reason for anyone to believe that throwing the switch will be harmful, then it is plausible to say not only that B was without fault in throwing the switch but also that it was permissible for him to do so. For these reasons, I do not believe that the sense of 'ought not' that is directly linked with the moral impermissibility of actions is the objective sense.

An Agent's Reasons and the Meaning of an Action

Whether or not the agent's reasons for acting affect the permissibility of an action, the agent's reasons do affect what I will call the *meaning* of the action—the significance of this action for the agent and others. The expression cases I discussed above provide examples of this. My call to a sick relative has a different meaning for the recipient (and hence also for me), depending on the reason for which I call. It is one thing if I call because I am genuinely concerned about his welfare, another if I am indifferent to his welfare but want to please my wealthy grandfather by appearing to be concerned about my relatives, and yet another if I hate this relative and am calling to have the pleasure of hearing how weak he sounds. In each of these cases my call indicates something different about our relationship, and we have different reasons for valuing it, being disappointed by it, being ashamed of it, resenting it, cherishing it, or reacting to it in other ways.

The meaning of an action in the sense I am concerned with should be distinguished from a different sense in which the meaning of an action is determined by the reactions of others (or by the ways it would be reasonable for them to react). For example, if the only family in the neighborhood that was not invited to the block party is also the only black family in the neighborhood, then that family may reasonably take this as a sign of prejudice, even if they were left out by mistake, or because only people with children were invited and they have none. Effects like their reaction are important and can affect the permissibility of an action. Meaning in this broader sense is not a function of the agent's actual reasons. It is, rather, a matter of what others reasonably or unreasonably take those reasons to be. But meaning in this sense is not the focus of my inquiry, because my concern is with the ways in which an agent's reasons for acting can affect the permissibility of what he or she does.

In expression cases, actions have meaning in a narrow, almost linguistic sense. My call to my sick relative, for example, is intended to express a certain kind of concern—that is, to indicate that I am calling for certain reasons and want her to see that those are my reasons. But the meaning of an action in the sense I am concerned with is broader than this. If someone acts with no regard whatsoever for the interests of another person, then this has a certain meaning—it indicates something significant about his attitude toward that person and about their relationship with each other—whether or not it was his intention to convey this.[10]

I have said that the meaning of an action is its significance *for certain individuals,* because the same action performed for the same reasons can have different significance for different people, depending on their relation to the agent. For example, the fact that a person has made a large sacrifice because of her commitment to a certain cause has one kind of significance for others who are committed to that cause, a different meaning for beneficiaries of that cause, and a different meaning still for those who are committed to rival causes. As this example indicates, although some forms of meaning have to do with moral assessment, meaning is not necessarily moral. An action can have meaning because of what it indicates about the agent's degree of commitment to some aim, even if this commitment, such as attachment to a particular cultural tradition, is morally neutral—neither morally required or morally forbidden.

The phrase "the meaning of the action *for Jones*" could be taken to mean the significance that Jones sees the action as having. This is not, however, what I intend. By the meaning of an action for a person, I mean the significance that person has reason to assign to it, given the reasons for which it was performed and the person's relation to the agent. The significance of your action, for me, is thus something I can be mistaken about. I may regard your action as a betrayal, but I may be mistaken about this either because I misinterpret your reasons for acting as you did or because I have a mistaken idea of what I am entitled to demand of you, given our relationship.

The examples of meaning that I have given so far have concerned the significance of an agent's action for others, but actions obviously have meaning for their agents as well. The fact that I acted, say, with indifference to the needs of a friend, or failed to do what I could see was required by a value I take myself to be committed to, can have great significance for me—for my feelings about myself and my understanding of my relations with others. Similarly, on the positive side, I may rightly attach great significance to acting in ways that express my love of my family, or my commitment to a cause, and this gives me reason to value having opportunities to act in these ways.

The permissibility of an action and its meaning are interrelated. If it is impermissible for me to treat you in a certain way, then my treating you in that way has a certain meaning: it indicates a failure on my part to give proper weight to those considerations that make such treatment impermissible. But the meaning of an action can vary independently of its permissibility. Injuring you intentionally and negligently inflicting the same injury are both impermissible but have different meanings: the former reflects outright hostility to your interests, the latter only a lack of sufficient care.

I have said that the meaning of an action depends on the agent's reason for performing it. But an agent may see many considerations as bearing on an action, and may see more than one of them as sufficient to make that action worth undertaking. When this is so, all of the various ways in which the agent saw those considerations as bearing on the action can be relevant to its meaning. The meaning of an action does not depend on the agent's singling out one of these considerations as *the* reason for which he acts.

Suppose, for example, that I promised my friend that I would meet him for dinner, and that it is also true that I would greatly enjoy seeing him and that there is no other way I would rather spend my evening. I may regard each of these as an entirely sufficient reason for going to the restaurant at the appointed time. Given that I promised, I would go even if I did not feel like an evening out, and given how much I expect to enjoy it, I would go even if I had no obligation to do so. The meaning of the action for me and for my friend depends on the fact that I see both of these considerations as reasons for going. My turning up would have a different meaning if I went solely out of obligation or only because I thought it would be fun (giving no weight at all to the fact that I promised). Thus, given that I see both of these considerations as reasons, there is no need, for the purposes of determining the meaning of the act, to single out one of them as *the* reason for which I act. Doing so would change, and perhaps diminish, the meaning of the act. Moreover (and this is a point that will be important later), it is not clear what this "singling out" could consist in unless it involved changing my mind about whether one of the considerations was a relevant reason for taking this particular action.[11]

Doing the Right Thing for the Wrong Reason: Permissibility and Choice

I have been emphasizing the distinction between the deliberative use of principles and their critical use, to assess the way individuals decide what to do, and I have urged that we should distinguish between what moral principles require of an agent and the reasons on which that agent acts. But these distinctions may seem forced. It sounds odd to say that a person who completely ignores the moral reasons bearing on his action is behaving permissibly, even if what he does is "in accord with duty" and the effects of his action give no one ground for complaint. We do speak of people "doing the right thing but for the wrong reason," as when, for example, someone helps a person who is in dire need—perhaps even in danger of dying—but does so only as a way of getting her own name in the papers, rather than out of any concern for the person or for the fact that it would be wrong not to help. But is it clear that in such a case the agent acts permissibly?

The familiar example just mentioned is not the best for my present purposes. The agent's supposed aim in saving the person—enhancing her own reputation—will be achieved only if she appears to be acting from non-self-interested reasons. This makes what she does an instance of what I have called "expressive" action, open to moral criticism on the grounds that it is hypocritical. To consider a case in which the morally problematic character of the action cannot be explained in this way, suppose instead that the agent hates the person who needs help and would be happy to see him die, but she saves him anyway because she does not want him to die *right then,* since that would mean that his heir, with whom she is locked in a bitter political contest, would have much more money to spend on his campaign.

On the one hand, it would seem odd to say that saving the person for this reason is impermissible. What is an agent supposed to do in such a situation, *not* save the person? On the other hand, it might be said that helping for the wrong reason and not helping at all are not the only alternatives: what she *ought* to do is to help him for the *right* reason. There is a clear sense in which, if she does not do this, she is not treating the person in the way he is entitled to be treated. Moreover, it might be added, this should be clear to the agent at the time she is deliberating about what to do. Moral considerations are not esoteric or unknowable, like the facts in Day's End. A person who acts with no regard for the relevant moral considerations is certainly open to some kind of moral criticism. If what she does is nonetheless permissible, what marks the difference between the question of permissibility and moral criticism of this wider form?

One possible answer is that there is no such difference—the fact that the person in our example would not be helping the person for the right reason counts against its permissibility but is outweighed in this case by the fact that the person's life is at stake. (I noted this possibility earlier, in the case of calling the sick relative.) I believe, however, that there is a more fundamental distinction here: the agent's failure to be moved by the right reason reveals a fault in him, but it does not count against the permissibility of his action. The best explanation of this distinction seems to me to lie in the close connection between permissibility and the guiding of choice.

The question of permissibility is the question, "May I do X?" which is typically asked from the point of view of an agent who is presented with a number of different ways of acting. The question is, which of these may one choose?[12] The question of permissibility thus applies only to alternatives between which a competent agent can choose.

This proposal leaves open the possibility that the considerations that the agent would be taking as reasons if he or she acted in a certain way can be relevant to the permissibility of so acting, provided that acting in that way, for those reasons, is something the agent can choose. We have seen in the expression and expectation cases one way in which this possibility can be realized: given that if an agent were to call her sick relative, she would be doing it only to stop her mother from nagging her rather than out of genuine concern for the relative, it may be impermissible for her to call, since doing so would be hypocritical. In such cases the choice condition I mentioned above is fulfilled: recognizing what her reasons would be for telephoning her sick relative, for example, the agent can perfectly well choose not to call. But we are now considering a different possibility. The suggestion is that it might be impermissible either to bring about a result with certain bad reasons in mind or to fail to bring it about at all, and that the only thing that would be permissible would be to bring it about for the right reasons. If I am correct about the connection between permissibility and choice, this makes sense only if acting for those different reasons is something the agent can choose to do. I do not believe that such a choice is possible.

There is of course one level at which we clearly do choose to act for certain reasons. Any action is guided by some aim, and in choosing to perform that action we are choosing to be so guided. In the life-saving case described above, for example, a person who chooses to save a drowning man chooses to be guided by the aim of getting him out of the water safely, and hence chooses to see the fact that an action would serve this purpose as a reason to take that action. But the present question concerns a different set of reasons: the reasons that an agent might have for adopting the aim of saving the man. One can adopt an end only if one sees some consideration as counting in favor of it, and it is at this most basic level that I do not think that we can *choose* what to see as reasons.

We are certainly responsible for what we take to be reasons. That is to say, we are open to criticism, including but not limited to moral criticism, for taking things to be reasons that are not and for failing to respond to things that are. But we do not, it seems to me, *choose* which things to take as ultimate reasons. We have to decide whether something is a reason or not—this is part of our being responsible. But deciding in such a case is not choosing, because it lacks the relevant element of free play. When one sees each of several courses of action as supported by sufficient reasons, one can choose which of them to take. In this sense one can choose which reasons to act on. But, as I pointed out above in discussing the meaning of my meeting my friend for dinner, when one sees several considerations as counting in favor of the same action, one cannot choose to act on one of them rather than another unless one downgrades some of the reasons by changing one's mind about whether they really do count (or count sufficiently) in favor of the action in question. Changing one's mind in this way is a judgment—a decision—but not a *choice*. Holding constant one's judgment about which considerations count in favor of an action, there is no such thing as choosing, or "singling out," one of these as *the* reason that one is acting on.

One can, of course, choose to bring it about, or try to bring it about, that one regards or does not regard certain things as reasons. I can choose to direct my critical attention in such a way as to undermine my tendency to regard my rival's pain as something to be sought. And I can choose to direct my attention away from the faults of some morally dubious institution with which I am associated, so that I will continue to think that I have reason to promote its flourishing. It can thus be impermissible to do these things, or impermissible not to. But what I choose in these cases is not to see or not see certain things as reasons, but to undertake a process of self-manipulation aimed at bringing it about that I have such attitudes.[13]

This conclusion about choice and reasons explains why it is odd to say, in the case of the person who thinks that the only good reason to save a person is the advantage to her of that person's staying alive, that the only permissible course of action for her is to save the person for the right reason. Saying this is odd because it presupposes that it is open to her to choose to act out of concern for the person's well-being. It is open to her to choose whether to save the person or not, but not open to her to choose to see a certain consideration as a reason for doing so.[14] Therefore, according to the hypothesis we are considering, the question of permissibility applies only to the decision whether to save.[15]

This explanation may seem to be at odds with the very appealing idea that moral considerations are not esoteric but are available to any agent. If the reasons that a moral principle identifies as relevant are "available" in this sense, why is acting on them—doing the right thing for the *right* reason—not also available to the agent? The answer is that the availability of moral considerations simply means that a normally competent agent ought to be able to understand them and see that they provide reasons. It does not follow that an agent who, for whatever reason, does not see the force of such a reason is nonetheless in a position to *choose* to see its force, or to act on it. Only the latter is denied by the hypothesis I have offered.

Intention and the Claims of Agents

I return now to the general question of how the permissibility of an action can depend on the meaning of that action or, more broadly, on the agent's reasons for so acting. Expression and expectation cases have already provided examples of the dependence of permissibility on meaning, but the dependence in those cases is derivative—depending on other moral principles requiring openness about one's aims. The predictive significance of intention, although important, is also derivative, depending ultimately on the significance of the effects that an action can be expected to have on others. So the question remains whether permissibility can depend on meaning, or on an agent's reasons for action, in a more direct and fundamental way. I will separate my inquiry into two parts. First, in this section and the following one, I will investigate whether the meaning of an action and the agent's reasons for performing it can have, as it were, a positive effect on the case for the permissibility of an action, by strengthening the agent's case for being permitted to so act. Second, in the two subsequent sections I will consider whether the meaning of an action, and the agent's reasons for performing it, can count against its permissibility by strengthening the objections that others have to such an action.

    The case for the moral permissibility of doing X under

conditions C depends on the reasons that someone in those conditions would have for doing X. So there is one sense in which it is obviously true that the permissibility of an action depends on the agent's reasons for doing it. But what is obviously true is that the permissibility of an action depends on the reasons that a person in that situation *actually has* for so acting. It does not immediately follow from this that it is permissible for a person to act in this way *only* if he or she is actually acting for the reasons that support this permission. It is this latter claim that is my present concern.

One class of cases in which this claim does follow are instances of what I called above the predictive significance of intent. Suppose that my house is on fire, and that the only way I can get to a source of water to put it out is by crossing your land. If, as I will assume for purposes of argument, this reason for crossing your land makes it permissible for me to do so, what it makes permissible is my crossing your land in order to get (that is to say, with the aim of getting) water to fight the fire. It does not make it permissible for me to cross your land just to see it, or to get water for my flowers, leaving my house to burn. (And it does not permit this even if I am strangely more interested in inspecting your land, or watering my flowers, than I am in saving my house.) What justifies the limitation on your property rights is the importance of saving my house. Thus it matters whether my crossing your land is actually instrumental in fighting my fire, which it would not be if I simply walked around gawking at your enormous house, or brought back only enough water for my flowers.[16] But so long as I need the water to put out the fire, I need to cross your land to get it, and I accomplish this purpose by doing so, my actual state of mind is irrelevant. The permissibility of what I do in this case does not depend on whether I am also motivated by the other aims just mentioned, or on which of these is my "real reason" for crossing your land. (As I have argued above, there may be no answer to the latter question.)

So the significance of intent in these cases is, again, predictive. The question then becomes whether there are cases in which the significance of an agent's reasons for acting goes beyond this—whether the reasons that move an agent to action can be relevant to permissibility when the consequences of the action are held constant.

An example of a promise can serve to bring out the question. Suppose that A is renting an apartment to B. A promises B that so long as he is a good tenant (pays the rent on time, takes good care of the property, and so on) she will not evict him unless she needs the apartment for one of her children. But suppose that after a few years A comes to be irritated with B and would prefer not having him around. It also happens that her daughter needs a place to live, and she asks A about the apartment. Although A is not eager to have her daughter as a tenant, she decides that on balance this would be less bad than being stuck with B. So she gives B notice and rents the apartment to her daughter instead. I assume that A feels some obligation to help her daughter but is moved also by her irritation with B. If she liked B better, she would probably have refused her daughter's request.

Does the permissibility of what A does in this case depend on the relative role of these two reasons in her decision?

It seems to me that it does not. So long as A's daughter needs a place to live, A has the option of evicting B to meet this need. This conclusion is supported by a plausible analysis of the promise A made to B. The aim of that promise was to provide B with assurance that he would not be evicted at will, while reserving for A the opportunity to meet her familial obligations. Things might be different if we took the point of the promise to be guaranteeing A the chance to engage in an action with a certain *meaning*—an action done out of parental love or duty. In that case the exception to the promise would apply only if A was in fact moved in this way. But this construal of the promise would make A seem oddly self-absorbed.

Since this case depends on the content of a particular promise, it would not in any event be a case in which an agent's reasons had fundamental moral significance. So let's consider another case in which the issue is not the content of a particular promise but the limits of the moral requirement of fidelity to promises.[17] Suppose that you live in California, and you promised some time ago to attend the wedding of some old friends, which will be held in New York. Three weeks before the wedding, however, you learn that you have cancer, and your doctor urges you to have surgery immediately and then begin a course of chemotherapy, which would make it impossible for you to travel to the wedding. I assume that this gives you more than sufficient reason not to make the trip. Suppose, however, that you would like very much to see your friends and would make the trip despite the doctor's recommendation were it not for the fact that one of the actors from your favorite soap opera will be making a personal appearance in your town that week and you don't want to miss the chance to see him. Is it still permissible for you not to go, given that this would be your reason for not doing so?

It seems to me that it is permissible. The threat to your life releases you from any obligation to make the trip. But it is important here to separate the question of permissibility from a question of meaning. The fact that you care more about seeing a soap opera star than you do about your friends' wedding says something about your relationship with them. Friendship would not require you to risk your life to be at their wedding, but it would normally involve caring more about your friends than about seeing a famous stranger. Your reason for failing to make the trip would therefore give rise to a reasonable question in your friends' minds about their relationship with you. But this question is about the priorities that your choice reveals rather than about whether you have violated a moral obligation.

Intention and the Permissibility of Self-Defense

The factors we have considered so far can also explain the scope of the permission to act in self-defense. Aquinas's discussion of this question is often cited as one of the origins of the doctrine of double effect.[18] In his account, the permissibility of homicide in self-defense turns importantly on the intention of the agent—specifically on whether and in what way the agent is aiming at his or her own survival and at the death or injury of the person who threatens it. This makes it particularly relevant to consider here what role the agent's intention plays on the account I am offering, and how that role is explained.

The permissibility of self-defense is an exception to the general principle barring action that can be expected to cause death or grave injury to others. Two lines of argument support this exception. One is based on the idea that by threatening someone's life, agents undermine their standing to complain if force is used against them. How can someone who has, without justification, chosen to attack another person complain if force is used to repel that attack? The other line of argument is based on the great importance for a person of doing what is necessary to prevent loss of life or serious injury. How can anyone be asked to accept a principle barring them from taking such action, if the harm it would cause to others is not disproportionate? I will set aside the first line of argument and concentrate on the second, since it is here that the agent's intentions may be relevant.

The permission to use force in self-defense can be justified only when an agent reasonably believes that he or she is in danger and that force is necessary to protect against this danger. The permission can therefore license only such force as is reasonable for the agent to believe necessary to alleviate the threat. One difference between an agent who is moved only by the aim of self-protection and an agent who is moved by the aim of killing his hated rival is that the latter aim, but not the former, could move the agent to inflict greater injury than is required for self-protection.

This difference in intent can thus have predictive significance of the sort noted in my discussion of tactical bombing versus terror bombing. In that case, the question was the permissibility of approving a bombing mission. The intention of those who would carry out the mission was important because it was relevant to assessing what they would do when presented with unforeseen changes in circumstances. If, in permitting self-defense, we are licensing courses of action that may be carried out in different ways, the predictive significance of intent remains important.

But it is natural, in considering the permissibility of self-defense, to think of the permissibility of more specific actions, which involve specific risks of harm, such as stabbing or shooting the aggressor in a certain part of the body, or pushing him or her off a cliff. It may not be certain exactly what harm will be caused by such an action, but those consequences do not depend on further choices by the agent, hence not on the aims that would guide him or her. The permissibility of a specific action of this kind therefore depends only on whether it is reasonable for the agent to believe that such a use of force is *necessary* to avert a threat of death or grave bodily harm to himself—that no action that involved less risk of harm to the aggressor would suffice. If this condition is fulfilled, then the use of force is permissible. There is thus no need to consider the agent's reason for acting.

One can imagine a case in which the decision to engage in self-defense is more like the decision to authorize a bombing campaign. Suppose that to preserve one's life one must enter into an all-out physical struggle with the threatening person. One may know that as blows are struck in the course of the struggle, passions will rage, and that one may then strike out wildly in anger and hatred, using more force than necessary. This is especially likely if the assailant is someone one hates. What is one supposed to do in such a case, however? Passively submit and allow oneself to be killed? The permissibility of fighting may be more obvious in the case of a "guilty threat," a person who has chosen to attack someone. But suppose the attacker is in the grip of drug-induced paranoia, for which he is not at all at fault. It might be noble in such a case to avoid fighting, because once the fight has begun one might be drawn into using more force than necessary. But is this required? I do not see that it is. Even in this case, it is not clear that the permissibility of using force in self-defense depends on the agent's intent.

Moreover, the question of what "the agent's reason" is for engaging in a particular use of force may have no determinate answer. Any agent who reasonably believes that a certain use of force is necessary to avert death or grave bodily harm sees that he or she has reason to use force in this way. Such a person may also be moved by hatred, and by a desire to kill the person who presents the threat. But as I have argued above, there may be no answer to the question of which motive is predominant, and the permissibility of the action does not depend on answering it, so long as these other conditions are fulfilled.

Intention and the Claims of Others: Discrimination

I turn now to cases in which an agent's reasons for acting may affect the permissibility of her action by strengthening the reasons that others have to object to such acts. Acts of discrimination provide plausible examples of this kind. There may be cases in which it would be permissible for an agent to fail to give a person a certain benefit, but not permissible to do so *because*, for example, he or she belongs to a racial group the agent regards as inferior or not worthy of the kind of consideration that others are owed.

One way of conceiving such a case is to suppose that the agent is under an obligation (perhaps in virtue of having taken on some role) to distribute a benefit according to certain criteria. This might be, for example, an obligation to hire the person who is most qualified to perform a certain job. In such a case it would be wrong for the agent to refuse to give the job to the best-qualified person because of that person's race. But, given the obligation we have assumed the agent to have, the wrongfulness of that action can be explained without appeal to the discriminatory nature of the agent's reasons. It would also be wrong to give the job to a friend or relative rather than to the best-qualified person, or to assign the job without considering the qualifications of various candidates at all because this seemed like too much work. These would not be cases of discrimination.

The wrongs involved in cases of this kind can be explained on two levels. First, substantively, it may be wrong to give the job to a certain person because someone else, who is better qualified, has a stronger claim to it. Second, procedurally as it were, such an action can be wrong because the agent has not taken the steps needed to find and attend to the information that is relevant to making a correct decision. This fault is like a kind of recklessness, a failure to take due care. It would apply even if the person whom the agent selected (after not even looking at the applications) just happened to be the best-qualified candidate. What we are trying to identify here, however, is a kind of discrimination that is wrong for reasons that go beyond these objections—that has to do with the objectionable character of the agent's positive reasons for choosing some candidates over others.

To see how a discriminatory reason can be essential to the wrongfulness of what an agent does, we should look for a case in which it is open to the agent to distribute a good to any one of several different people, *so long as* she does not do so for the wrong kind of reason. It may seem, for example, that it would be morally permissible for someone to rent her house to any one of several prospective tenants but not morally permissible to refuse to rent it to one of those people because of his race.

Prejudicial action of this kind seems morally objectionable, but what is the basis of this objection? Why is it morally impermissible to decide among prospective tenants on certain grounds, such as race, but not on other grounds, such as that they went to Princeton, or they wear clothing in colors that clash?

One possible answer would be that, at least at the most fundamental level of explanation, there is no important difference between these reasons. The idea would be that the fundamental moral idea at work in these cases is a perfectly general idea of fairness, according to which everyone is entitled to an equal chance at important goods such as housing. This means that they are entitled to be judged on the basis of their suitability as tenants (whether they can be relied upon to pay rent promptly, keep the premises clean, not be noisy, and so on). If there is no way to choose between prospective tenants on these grounds, then one should hold a lottery, giving each an equal chance, or make a decision on some other impartial basis, such as who applied first. This would bring all discriminatory action within the scope of a generalized version of the explanation I considered in the case of a specific obligation to distribute a benefit on certain grounds. As in that case, the basis of the wrong would lie in the superior claims of others, or in the failure to use the proper procedure to decide between these claims.

This account seems unsatisfactory on a number of grounds. First, the basic demand on which it is based seems overly strict and moralistic. It does not seem, to me at least, that we are morally required to flip a coin to choose between prospective tenants with the same substantive qualifications. Second, even if there is a moral requirement of this kind, there seems to be something particularly objectionable about discrimination on racial grounds. We are looking for an explanation of why this is so.

A second possible explanation would be that the decisions that we call discriminatory are objectionable because they involve a kind of insult—an expression of the view that certain people are inferior or socially unacceptable. There is something right about this. Discrimination, as we commonly understand it, does seem to involve a judgment of this kind. But prejudices of the other kinds I have mentioned (against Ivy League graduates, or people who dress in a certain way) may also involve such judgments, and can therefore also be insulting. What needs to be explained is why discrimination on racial grounds, and perhaps certain other grounds, is more serious, and therefore wrong.

One thing that seems crucial to racial discrimination in particular is that the prejudicial judgments it involves are not just the idiosyncratic attitudes of a particular agent but are widely shared in the society in question and commonly expressed and acted on in ways that have serious consequences. Many of the petty likes and dislikes of our fellow citizens may be things we just have to live with. But it is another matter when the view that members of a certain group are inferior, and not to be associated with, becomes so widely held in a society that members of that group are denied access to important goods and opportunities. The basis of the wrong of discrimination lies in the moral objection to this kind of harm. No one can be asked to accept a society that marks them out as inferior in this way and denies them its principal benefits. When this occurs, individual acts of discrimination on certain grounds become impermissible because they support and maintain this practice. They are thus wrong because of their consequences—the exclusion of some people from important opportunities—and because of their meaning—the judgment of inferiority that they express and thereby help to maintain.

The latter objection, because it depends on the meaning of an action, depends on the agent's reasons. But the former does not. Once a practice of discrimination exists, decisions that deny important goods to members of the group discriminated against—and do so without sufficient justification—are wrong even if they express no judgment of inferiority on the agent's part. They are wrong even if made simply out of laziness, or out of a desire to avoid offending others by going against established custom.

It is worth noting that this idea of discrimination is unidirectional. It applies only to actions that disadvantage members of a group that has been subject to widespread denigration and exclusion: in the case of race, it applies to actions or policies that disadvantage blacks, not to all policies that employ race-based criteria. So when discrimination is understood in this way, "reverse discrimination" is an oxymoron. If there is an objection to affirmative action policies, it must be based on some other grounds, such as the claim that there is a uniquely correct basis for allocating the benefits in question, to which race is irrelevant. This claim needs to be supported by defending the criteria in question rather than by appeal to the idea of discrimination, since, as I pointed out at the beginning of this section, not all deviations from relevant criteria are open to the charge of discrimination.

Intention and the Claims of Others: Threats

Not all threats are impermissible, but the fact that a certain action is a threat can be a moral objection to it, and it may seem that actions are sometimes impermissible because of their coercive character. Whether a course of action is a threat seems to depend on the agent's intent (specifically, on his or her reasons for adopting this course of action). So this seems to be a class of cases in which permissibility may depend on intent. To see whether and how intent can be relevant to permissibility in such cases we need to consider, first, what makes an action a threat rather than, say, merely a warning.[19]

Threats and warnings are alike in one important respect: each involves telling a person that acting in a certain way will lead to unwanted consequences. One way in which a warning can fail to be a threat is if the speaker has no control over the unwanted consequence. Warning someone that leaning on a boulder is likely to cause an avalanche is not a threat. But telling someone that if he acts in a certain way then you will do something he does not want you to do is not necessarily a threat either. Suppose I tell you that if you give a course in ethics next year, rather than your usual course on metaphysics, then I will give a course on metaphysics myself. This could be a warning, if I believe that you don't want me to teach metaphysics, given my neopositivist tendencies. But this warning would not be a threat if, for example, my reason for intending to give a metaphysics course if you do not is just that I believe that such a course should be offered every year.

For my telling you of my intention to do something to be a threat, it is necessary, at the least, that I intend to do this— and tell you of my intention—because I think that this is something you will not like. It is not necessary that I have any thought that telling you this will influence your behavior. I might be seeking revenge, in threatening you, or just expressing spite. But the class of threats that I am concerned with, which I will call incentive threats, are ones that attempt to influence the recipient's behavior.[20]

Whether something is a threat, or an incentive threat, thus depends on the agent's reasons: not just on her reasons for communicating her intention to act a certain way but also on her reasons for forming that intention to begin with. The question I am interested in is whether and why this difference in an agent's reasons should make a difference to the permissibility of what he or she does.

Considered abstractly, an incentive threat has the following structure. The recipient of the threat is in a position to choose between doing A and doing B, each with certain consequences. But the intervener, to get the recipient to choose B rather than A, decides (and announces to the recipient) that if the recipient does A, the intervener will alter the consequences of A by bringing about something—call it the penalty—that the recipient has good reason not to want.

When nonincentive threats are impermissible, this impermissibility is mostly explained by the impermissibility of inflicting the penalty. If it would be permissible for me to do P (whether you like it or not), the fact that I do P because you will not like it does not make my doing this, or telling you that I will do it, impermissible. My reason for doing P changes the meaning of my action—gives it an "in your face" character—but does not change its permissibility. The impermissibility of a nonincentive threat can be explained on the ground that if it is impermissible to do something to a person, then it is impermissible to give him good grounds for fearing that you are going to do it.

In the case of impermissible incentive threats, however, things seem slightly different. At least in familiar "Your money or your life!" examples, the penalty itself is something that it is impermissible for the intervener to bring about. But there seems to be a moral objection to the threat that goes beyond the objections that apply to inflicting the threatened penalty, an objection that has to do with the fact that the recipient of the threat is being forced to do something. The question is how this further moral objection, which depends on the intent to influence, is best understood.

We might explain the wrongfulness of incentive threats

by saying that the recipient's choice situation is made worse by having the alternative of doing A encumbered by the unwanted penalty, or even by being put in the position of believing, falsely, that it is so encumbered. It is not always a bad thing to have undesirable effects attached to certain choices. Sometimes we need and benefit from encouragement to do things that we have good reason to do but might fail to do, given the unencumbered choice.[21] I should not object to the buzzer that annoys me until I put on my seat belt, or the law that threatens me if I drive while intoxicated, since these may be good things from my point of view. It can, however, be a bad thing for someone to have a previously desirable alternative rendered undesirable by having some undesirable consequence attached to it, and the fact that a threat does this might be what makes it morally objectionable, or even impermissible. But this objection to a threat does not depend on the intervener's intentions or her reasons for forming those intentions, which are the features that make it a *threat,* as opposed to a warning. Many things we do may worsen the choice situations of others, and the fact that they do so does not necessarily make them impermissible. So the fact that an incentive threat worsens the recipient's choice situation does not, in itself, explain why it would be impermissible.

We should, however, consider in more detail the ways in which an incentive threat can change the recipient's choice situation. One of these ways has to do with meaning. By changing the reasons the recipient has for doing A and for doing B, the penalty attached to A changes the recipient's choice situation by changing the meaning of the recipient's doing A and of his doing B. This is so even in nonthreat cases, in which the "penalty" is attached by nature. If sailing to my destination is made dangerous by high winds and rough seas, this not only makes that alternative less desirable but also changes the meaning of my choices. Deciding to get there another way can now be interpreted as a response to the danger, and hence as prudent, or as an unseemly backing down in the face of danger, or as indicating a lack of confidence in my seamanship.

Effects of this kind are more pronounced when the penalty is attached by another agent with the aim of influencing the recipient's actions. In a case of sexual harassment during a job interview, for example, in the absence of a threat, the recipient can choose between having sex with the prospective employer or not. But once a threat has been made, what the job applicant can decide is whether or not to have *coerced* sex with the employer, which is something quite different. In addition, the alternative of taking the job now involves going to work for someone who has treated one (or tried to treat one) in this way, and declining it could be seen as an assertion of one's dignity. More generally, whatever action A may be, the threat to attach a penalty to the recipient's doing A changes the alternative of doing A into the alternative of doing A in defiance of this threat, and adds to action B the character of giving in to the intervener and being "pushed around" by him or her.

So here is one way in which the distinction between incentive threats and warnings—and hence the intervener's reasons for doing what he or she does—becomes relevant. Considering just the badness, for the recipient, of having alternative A available only at the price of a certain penalty, there would seem to be no difference between the intervener's threatening to inflict the penalty if the recipient does A and her merely warning him that she has this conditional intention, as in the example of curricular planning. In either case, the alternative of doing A is made less appealing by the same price. The difference lies in the intervener's reasons for forming the conditional intention of inflicting the penalty if the recipient does A. Incentive threats and warnings have different meanings, and therefore different effects on the meanings of the alternative actions open to the recipient.

The meaning of an incentive threat, and its effect on the meanings of the actions available to the person threatened, also vary with the relationship between the intervener and the recipient and with the intervener's reasons for wanting to influence the recipient's actions. It is one thing to be threatened by a parent, another by a teacher; one thing to be threatened by one's boss, another by a coworker. It makes a difference as well if the threat is issued for what the intervener sees as the recipient's own good or to advance some cause that the intervener and recipient share, or if the threat is made simply for the intervener's personal gain or just for the pleasure of wielding power.[22] These differences in the meaning of the intervener's actions give rise to differences in the way the relations between intervener and recipient are affected by the threat.

These observations about the meaning-altering effects of incentive threats apply as well to offers, which are like incentive threats except that the "penalty" is something that, considered in itself, the recipient has reason to want. If someone offers me a lot of money if I do B rather than A, this changes the meaning of my choices. B might have been something that I had only altruistic reasons for doing. Once the offer is made, my reasons for doing B are mixed, and doing A now involves passing up a lot of money. These effects also depend on my relationship with the intervener, and on his or her reasons for making the offer: as before, it makes a difference if the offer comes from a parent, or from an anonymous benefactor, and whether it is made for what the intervener judges to be my own good, or to advance some other project that he or she may have.

Recipients may have good reason to object to changes of these kinds in the meaning of the actions available to them, and therefore good reason to object to others' intervening in their lives in these ways. I believe that these meaning-based objections explain a good deal of what is distinctively objectionable about threats, and may in some cases be so serious as to make some incentive threats (or even offers) impermissible. But the moral objections to other incentive threats—the robber's "Your money or your life!" comes to mind—seem to go beyond this. So we need to look further.

Someone who issues an incentive threat has two intentions that may be impermissible. One is the intention to inflict the penalty if the recipient does not comply with the threat. The other is, if the recipient does comply, to benefit from some action, B, on the part of the recipient. The threat is necessary because the recipient would not do B in the absence of the threat. I will proceed on the hypothesis, which seems to me very plausible, that if the threat is impermissible, then the objection to it must lie in an objection to one or both of these courses of action.[23] Since we are looking for objections to a threat that go beyond objections to the threatened action itself, we should look at the second course of action, which involves "forcing" the recipient to do something.

This line of thought is initially promising. In many cases in which incentive threats are clearly impermissible, the thing that the intervener wants the recipient to do involves a form of interaction that requires the recipient's consent. The intended effect of the threat is to secure the recipient's acquiescence in this interaction, but the problem, we might say, is that in the presence of the threat this acquiescence does not amount to consent of the required kind. This is clear in the case of robbery. Because of the robber's threat to kill the recipient, her handing over the money does not confer title to it. That is why it is robbery. Similarly, we might say that an employer's threat to fire an employee if she does not engage in sex with him is impermissible because this threat renders the proposed sexual encounter nonconsensual.

But not all incentive threats have this consent-undermining character. My employer may prefer not to pay me more, but it is not impermissible for me to threaten to quit unless he does. If he gives me a raise as a result of this threat, his consent to the raise has legitimating force. When I take the money, it is not robbery.

This example reminds us that the intent to influence, which is the defining characteristic of incentive threats, is not in itself a mark of impermissibility. It also supports the hypothesis that the impermissibility of a threat depends on whether it renders the recipient's response in some way invalid. So we need to consider when a threat has this effect, and whether this may depend on the agent's reasons for issuing the threat.

One natural suggestion would be that a threat has this delegitimizing effect if it renders the recipient's participation in the interaction involuntary. But "involuntariness" cannot be seen as simply a matter of the recipient's will being "forced" or a matter of the unattractiveness of the alternative, given the severity of the penalty. To render the intervener's interaction with the recipient impermissible, a threat need not impair the recipient's rational faculties or prevent him or her from making a choice. In most cases, the recipient of an impermissible threat still chooses what to do; he or she simply faces a different choice. Whether the threat deprives the recipient's acquiescence of the licensing power of consent is not settled merely by the magnitude of the penalty, or by the recipient's degree of reluctance in doing B in the face of it. A person's degree of reluctance in handing over a large sum of money to avoid immediate and painful death, and the unattractiveness of the alternative he faces, might be the same whether the person requiring this money is a robber or a surgeon who will perform a difficult operation.

What distinguishes these cases? A plausible hypothesis seems to me this: a threat renders the recipient's consent invalid just when it is a threat the agent is entitled to make. That is to say, just when it would be permissible for the agent to inflict the threatened penalty if the recipient did not comply. This hypothesis seems to explain the examples we have considered so far. The robber's threat, "Your money or your life!" renders the resulting transaction nonconsensual, because the robber is not entitled to kill the recipient if he does not hand over the money. The surgeon's demand for payment *is* valid, and the patient's payment consensual, if the surgeon is entitled to refuse to operate if not paid what she asks. Similarly, my threat to quit if I do not receive a raise is permissible, and my employer's acquiescence consensual, because it is permissible for me to quit if not paid more.

This way of explaining the cases makes the permissibility of the course of action in which the recipient complies with a threat, and hence the permissibility of the threat itself, depend on the permissibility of the course of action in which the recipient defies the threat and the agent inflicts the penalty. The permissibility of the threat will thus depend on the agent's reasons only if the permissibility of carrying out the threat depends on those reasons.

This does not appear to be the situation in any of the cases I have just been considering. What matters in these cases is whether the person who makes the threat would have sufficient justification for carrying it out, not on the reasons that would move him to do so. For example, if I am underpaid and the raise I asked for is reasonable, then I would be justified in quitting if I did not receive it, even if my actual reason for quitting was to annoy the boss. Things are not so clear in the case of sexual harassment, however.

The explanation I am considering for the permissibility of a threat would imply that an employer's threat to fire an employee unless she has sex with him is impermissible, and the resulting interaction nonconsensual, only if it would be impermissible for the employer to fire her if she did not comply with the threat. But suppose that business is bad, the employer has to reduce his staff, and there is no business-related reason to fire one employee rather than another. He would thus be justified in firing any one of several employees, including the one in question. If this is so, then there is a sense in which it would be permissible for the employer to fire the employee if she does not comply with his demand. To decide that this is not the case, and thus support the conclusion that his threat is impermissible, we must take the phrase "permissible to fire her if she did not comply with his threat" to mean "permissible to fire her *because* she did not comply with his threat" and claim that this action would not be permissible. This would make the permissibility of the threat depend on the agent's reasons for carrying it out rather than just on whether he would be justified in doing so.

The fact that sex is involved adds to the force of the example, but the case would have the same structure if we supposed that the employer demanded money (that is, a bribe), or demanded that the employee wash his cars or mow his grass or run personal errands for him. These examples belong to a wider class of what might be called abuse-of-privilege cases. Their common structure is this: There is good reason for individuals in certain positions to be entitled to give or withhold goods or opportunities that are important to others. But if this privilege is unrestricted—if these individuals could give or withhold these goods for any reasons whatever—this would give them an unacceptable form of control over others.

This discretion must therefore be constrained. If the constraint is to be defined by specifying the reasons for which agents may give or withhold these goods, this might be done either positively or negatively. The positive strategy would state the reasons for which it would be permissible to with-hold the goods in question, reasons that flow from the case for giving such agents discretionary control over these goods in the first place. So, for example, we might specify that employ-ers can fire employees only for reasons having to do with the success of the enterprise in question. As the sexual harassment example shows, however, these reasons may be indeterminate. If it is permissible to fire *someone* when these reasons are in-determinate, but some such firings are impermissible, then the distinction between permissible and impermissible firing must be specified in some other way. So we might switch to the neg-ative strategy and specify that the employer may not fire one employee rather than another for certain kinds of reasons, such as reasons of personal advantage. This would seem to cover demands for bribes as well as for sexual favors and other kinds of services. But this way of specifying illicit reasons may be too broad. Is it, for example, permissible for an employer to fire one employee rather than another because he finds the lat-ter a more appealing person?

To answer this question we need to look at the matter from the point of view of the employee and ask whether being "appealing" or "agreeable" in the relevant way is something that can reasonably be demanded of an employee as a condi-tion of employment. This makes a more general conclusion apparent: Although we may specify the distinction between permissible and impermissible exercises of discretionary con-trol over important goods (and hence between permissible and impermissible threats to withhold those goods) by speci-fying the reasons on which agents may or may not act, the dis-tinction between permissible and impermissible reasons has a deeper explanation. What is morally basic is not a class of reasons that it is inherently illegitimate for agents to act on but, rather, the reasonable claims of victims that these agents' discretion to give or withhold important goods should not be defined so broadly as to make them unjustifiably subject to the agents' control.

Of course, what counts as "unjustifiable" forms of control will depend on the reasons for granting the discretionary powers in question as well as the reasons that others have for wanting these powers to be limited. I have taken employment decisions as examples because these are cases in which it is easy to identify the reasons supporting the relevant power: easy, that is, to say that considerations of efficiency that justify the discretionary powers of employers do not justify defining those powers so broadly as to allow employers to fire workers for any reason at all. Moreover (and this is what is crucial) powers defined so broadly that they could be used to extract money or other favors from employees would make employees unacceptably subject to their employers' control.[24] I believe that this analysis generalizes beyond the case of employment to cover the wider range of threats that I have called "abuses of privilege." A threat of this kind is permissible only when the person who makes it is entitled to inflict the penalty or refrain from doing so depending on whether the recipient fails to comply with the threat or complies with it.

To summarize: Whether an action is a threat depends on the agent's intentions and reasons for forming those intentions. The fact that an action is a threat affects its meaning, and a threat affects the meaning of the actions available to its recipients. (Offers can have similar effects.) These differences in meaning capture much of what is morally distinctive about threats. But the permissibility of a threat generally depends on whether the agent is entitled to inflict the penalty in question. It is natural to describe the class of impermissible threats in terms of the illegitimacy of the agent's reasons. But the illegitimacy of these reasons is explained by the claims of those who are victims of threats to be free from certain forms of control.

Conclusion

Chapter 1 had two positive theoretical aims: to introduce the distinction between two ways in which a moral principle can be applied, and to identify clearly the idea of permissibility. With respect to intention, its aim was mainly negative: to explain away the idea that the agent's aims in acting are relevant to the permissibility of an action in the way claimed by the doctrine of double effect. My aim in this chapter has been more positive: to identify and explain the ways in which an agent's reasons for action can be relevant to the permissibility of what he or she does. I have identified two main ways in which this can be so. First, an agent's reasons have predictive significance, as determinants of the likely consequences of the proposed course of action. Second, the reasons for which an agent is acting affect what I have called the meaning of the action, and in some cases the meaning of an action can affect its permissibility. (Expression and expectation cases are examples of this, but not the only ones.)

The main theoretical aim of this chapter has been to introduce and explain the distinction between the permissibility

of an action and its meaning, a distinction that will be important in the following chapters. Some may question whether
the meaning of an action and its moral permissibility can be
separated as clearly as I have been supposing. Morality not
only tells us to treat others in certain ways—to refrain from
harming them, for example—but also gives us certain reasons
for doing so. It tells, us, for example, that their interests matter,
and that we should take these interests as providing reasons.
People who are indifferent to the interests of other rational beings are open to moral criticism on this account, whether or
not they behave in ways that cause others harm or fail to help
them in ways that they should. Why, then, doesn't the question
of permissibility apply to the reasons for which an agent acts
as well as to the expected effects of that action? The answer I
have offered is that the question of permissibility arises only
with respect to alternatives between which an agent can
choose. Therefore, since it is not open to us to choose which
(ultimate) reasons to act on, a person who "does the right
thing, but for the wrong reason" may be doing something permissible even though he or she is open to moral criticism on
other grounds.

3

Means and Ends

The familiar Kantian formula, that rational agents must be treated as ends in themselves and not merely as means, seems to express an important moral truth. But it is not clear how this appealing formula should be understood. The phrases "treating someone as an end," "treating someone merely as a means," and "using someone" can be used to invoke a number of different ideas with apparent moral force. One of my aims in this chapter is to identify these ideas and assess their moral importance.

A second aim is more theoretical, and continues the theme of the earlier chapters. On any plausible construal, whether in acting a certain way I treated someone merely as a means, or treated him as an end, depends at least in part on the reasons I saw as governing my action. So if actions are sometimes impermissible because they involve treating someone merely as a means, the permissibility of these actions depends on the agent's reasons. To carry out the inquiry begun in the earlier chapters, I thus need to consider in what way the idea of treating people as ends in themselves, never merely as means, serves as a criterion of permissibility, and whether, understood as such a criterion, it makes the permissibility of an action depend on what the agent took to be reasons for so acting.

Kant thought that the injunction to treat rational beings always as ends in themselves and never merely as a means was one way of stating the fundamental principle of morality that underlies all of our moral duties. But the idea that it is objectionable to treat someone merely as a means has also seemed to many people, not necessarily Kantians, to characterize a specific category of wrongness. The charge, "You were just *using* me!" has particular moral force, and it seems appropriate in response to some wrongs but not to others. It does not, for example, seem the appropriate charge for me to level when I encounter the stranger who, when he saw that I was in danger of drowning, could easily have saved me by pulling the lever that would have summoned the rescue service, but instead turned away and continued his stroll along the beach. He may have wronged me, but he was not using me in any normal sense of that term.

In other cases the fact that someone was "used" or "treated merely as a means" may seem to explain why an action is wrong. Suppose, for example, that I get you to join me in a business enterprise by leading you to believe (falsely, as I well know) that it will be beneficial for you as well as for me. It seems appropriate to say in such a case that I am "using" you, and "treating you merely as a means," and this may seem, in addition, to explain why my treatment of you is wrong.

The wrongfulness of treating someone merely as a means might also seem to explain why it is wrong to throw a person off a bridge to stop a runaway train that will otherwise kill five, but not wrong to switch the train onto an alternate track where only one person will be killed. The former action, but not the latter, involves treating the person as a means, it may be said, because only in the former case is the harmful involvement of the person necessary to the agent's plan. This might be thought to mark the important moral difference between the two cases.

The first two sections of this chapter are devoted to the idea of treating humanity as an end in itself, as a general characterization of moral rightness. I will consider how this idea is best understood and whether it makes the permissibility of an action depend on the agent's reasons for performing it. Then in the following sections I will consider whether a more specific idea of just using someone, or treating someone as a mere means, explains why certain specific actions are wrong, as in cases of the kinds I have already mentioned.

Treating Someone as an End: Alternative Interpretations

How should we understand the idea of treating someone as an end in him- or herself, and the contrast between this and treating someone merely as a means? One possibility is that a mere means is something that has value only insofar as it is useful for some other purpose. The idea of "usefulness" may be overly restrictive, however. The more basic contrast is between derivative and nonderivative value, where being useful as a way of bringing about some end is only one way of having derivative value. So, generalizing slightly, we could say that to regard something merely as a means is to see it as having no value except for what may be conferred on it by some other value, and that seeing something as an end in itself is seeing it as having value that is not derived from any other source.

The idea of "value" is slightly misleading here, since it may suggest something that is "to be promoted" and makes other things valuable insofar as they help to promote it. I believe that this is an overly narrow conception of value.[1] But since it is a conception that has an influence on our thinking, it will be helpful to restate the distinction I have just made, replacing the idea of value with that of being a source of reasons. This yields the following formulation. To see something as an end in itself is to see it as a nonderivative source of reasons. To see something as a mere means is to see it as something that provides us with reasons only derivatively—that is to say, only insofar as the reasons are provided by something else.

This formulation puts us in a better position to capture what I believe Kant had in mind. When Kant said that we all regard our own rational nature as an end in itself, he did not mean only that we see it as something we have reason to preserve and promote. He did mean that, but he also meant that we see ourselves as having the power to make it the case that we have reason to promote other things, by choosing those things as our ends.[2] This idea is not well expressed in terms of "being a value," if a value is understood mainly as something there is reason to promote. Insofar as we have reason to promote the ends that a rational being has chosen, this is not because doing so is a way of promoting or preserving that rational being itself. So we can better capture Kant's idea of rational beings as ends in themselves by moving beyond the idea of an end's being something there is reason to promote to the idea of its being a nonderivative source of reasons.

It sounds plausible to say that in choosing something as an end we give it the status of something that can provide reasons to do what will promote it, thereby giving rise to reasons that we did not have before. I believe, however, that if this is true at all, it is true only to a very limited degree, much less than Kant and many Kantians have suggested. To see something as one's end is to see it as something one has reason to promote. But it does not follow that to see something as one's end is to see it as something one has reason to promote *because* it is one's end. In most cases, I believe, this is not true.[3] The reasons we have to promote our ends are just the features that gave us reason to make it an end in the first place.

The idea that by adopting something as our end we give ourselves a new reason to pursue it has greatest plausibility in what might be called tie-breaking cases. Suppose I have good reason to adopt any one of several goals, but not more than one of them (perhaps because they cannot be effectively pursued at the same time). If I adopt one of these goals, it would seem that I then have reason to do what will promote that goal, in a way that I do not have reason to do what will promote the alternative goals that were, before my decision, equally eligible. I believe that even in this special case it is a mistake to see the change in my practical situation as an instance of the power of a rational will to create reasons by adopting ends. But I will not pursue this question further here.[4]

Even if choosing something as our end does not give rise to new reasons to promote it, however, it can change things in other ways. First, it can make success in achieving that end something that contributes to our well-being. Second, as I have said, it makes that thing something that we must, insofar as we are not irrational, *see* as reason-giving. If something is our end, then we must (unless we are irrational) see ourselves as having reason to do what will promote it. But it does not follow that we in fact *have* reason to do those things. Whether we do or not depends on whether we have reason to have that end in the first place. If the end is utterly foolish, then what we have reason to do is to abandon it.

I believe Kant saw the idea that we all regard our own rational nature as having the power to confer reason-giving status on our ends as a very secure premise. He wanted to argue from this premise to the more controversial conclusion that we must see other people as having this same power, because they see themselves in this way "on the same basis that is rational for me."[5] In fact, however, the conclusion of this argument is more plausible than the premise. It is much more plausible to say that the fact that something is some *other* person's end can give rise to a reason for us to promote it, or at least not to interfere with it, than it is to say this in the case of our own ends. Indeed, I believe this claim is generally false as a claim about our own ends, whereas there is at least something to be said for it as a claim about the ends of others.

One reason why there is something to be said for it in their case is the fact that by making something their end, they may make success in achieving it a component of their well-being. Thus, insofar as we have reason to be concerned with their well-being, their making something their end gives us a reason to be concerned with it over and above whatever other reasons we may have. Concern for well-being is not the only factor at work here, however. Even if we judge that a person's end is not worth pursuing, and that he would be better off abandoning it, the fact that it *is* his end may give us reason to help him pursue it or, at least, reason not to interfere with his pursuit of it, out of respect for his autonomy as a person in charge of his own life.

It might be claimed that these factors are at work in our own case as well, but if true at all, this is true only to a much more limited degree than in the interpersonal case. By choosing something as our end, do we give rise to a new reason for trying to achieve it, namely that insofar as we achieve it we will have a more successful life? Perhaps, but this seems to me a somewhat special and self-absorbed kind of reason.[6] In any event it is not the kind of fundamental reason that Kant seemed to have in mind.

Nor does it seem, *in general,* that the reasons we have for pursuing the ends we have adopted flow from respect for our own autonomy. There are cases in which something like this may seem to be true. Suppose I have good reason to think that, many years from now, I will adopt ends that I now judge to be foolish. It may seem that the mere fact that these will be my ends gives me reason, now, to take measures to aid in my later pursuit of these ends, or at least reasons not to do what will interfere with this. But it is not clear to me to what extent this is so. What does seem clear is that, to the degree that it is so, it reflects special features of intertemporal planning. It may be that, in living a life, one has good reason to defer certain kinds of future decisions to one's judgment at that time. But this depends on the kind of judgments in question, and one's ability at that time to make them. When such reasons for deferral hold, they have weight against one's present judgment about the substantive merits of the ends in question. But these reasons derive from the special circumstances in question. What is revealed in such cases is not something that is true in every case: namely that by adopting an end we generate a reason for pursuing it.

There are also other reasons not to identify being an end in itself with having the power to confer positive value on other things by choosing them as ends. These reasons emerge when we consider what is involved in treating many different rational beings as ends in themselves. How are we supposed to decide what to do when we must choose between preserving some rational beings (or promoting their ends) and preserving other rational beings (or promoting *their* ends)?

If the idea that rational beings are ends in themselves meant just that we have nonderivative reason to preserve them and reason to promote their ends, then this idea would seem to place no limits on the degree to which some rational beings might be sacrificed to preserve others, or the ends of some sacrificed to promote the ends of others. This is the kind of maximizing consequentialist doctrine that many people have sought to avoid by appealing to the idea that we must treat others as ends in themselves, not merely as means. It seems far from what Kant had in mind.

So something more has to be said about what it is to be ends in ourselves and not mere means, if this idea is to provide an alternative to such consequentialist views. One possibility is to shift from the idea of rational beings having the power to confer positive value on things by choosing them as ends to an idea of rational beings as *legislating.* This has implications for the way in which we should proceed when there is a conflict between promoting the ends of some rational beings and promoting the ends of others. If rational beings merely have the power to generate reasons for pursuing things by choosing them as their ends, then it might seem that in cases of conflict we should simply balance those reasons against one another. But if respecting rational beings as ends in themselves is respecting them as legislators who must be able to authorize us to behave as we do, then what we should do instead is to ask what principles they would or could legislate for dealing with such situations.

I have described this as a shift, but for Kant (on at least one plausible interpretation) it represents no change. For him, on this interpretation, the power to confer value on ends is already understood as a power to make laws: in choosing an end, I must see myself as making a law for myself and for others about what is to count as a reason. Whether or not this is a plausible interpretation of what Kant says, I do not find it a very plausible view in itself. To adopt an end is to put that aim on one's "to do" list, so to speak. This might be described as adopting a plan or policy that involves doing it, and this in turn might be described more grandly as "giving oneself a law." But, as I have said, one need not see adopting an end as creating a reason to pursue it. The reasons I must see as reasons for doing what I have decided to do are the reasons I see as counting in favor of deciding to do it. Perhaps other people have a reason not to interfere with my plans, simply because they are my plans. But it does not seem that I am required to think that they do, simply as part of what I see myself as doing when I adopt the end.

So I do not think that, as rational agents, we must see ourselves and others as legislating what is and is not to count as a reason. But the idea that we should act only in ways that others could not reasonably refuse to authorize does seem to me a very appealing moral idea, and one that is seen as playing a fundamental role in our moral thinking. This idea can be interpreted in various ways. Kant wrote that one should act only on a maxim that one can at the same time will to be a universal law. I take this to mean that you should act on a maxim only if you can at the same time will that anyone who is inclined to act in this way should be permitted to do so. Derek Parfit has suggested it should mean that we ought to act on principles that everyone could rationally will to be universal laws.[7] I have proposed the related idea that actions are right only if there is a principle permitting them that no one could reasonably reject.[8] I will not pursue here the differences between these formulations, or their relative merits. I naturally have a preference for my own contractualist formula, and I will mainly rely on it in what follows, but the differences between these formulations will not matter.

Permissibility and Meaning

The various formulas I have just mentioned characterize, in a very abstract way, the distinction between permissible and impermissible action. My contractualist principle, for example, says that an action is impermissible if any principle that permitted it would be one that someone could reasonably reject. The idea that we should act in such a way as to treat rational beings as ends in themselves can also be read in this same way, as telling us that actions are impermissible if they are incompatible with the idea of rational beings as ends in themselves. But the idea of *treating* someone as an end in himself can also be read in a different way. On this reading, I treat someone as an end in herself only if I *take* the fact that she is an end in herself as giving me reasons to treat her in some ways but not others.

Read in this second way, Kant's formula is not a criterion of permissibility, since there are ways of failing to live up to it that do not involve doing anything impermissible. An example is Parfit's case of a gangster buying his morning coffee.[9] The gangster, Parfit supposes, does not regard the coffee seller as an end in himself, or as having any moral consequence whatever. He would not hesitate to kill him if it served his purposes. Nonetheless, whether because he enjoys his interaction with the coffee seller or just because he wants to avoid trouble, he treats the coffee seller fairly and politely as he buys his morning drink. The gangster does not treat the coffee seller as an end in himself in the second sense I just described; he treats him as a mere means. But what he does is not impermissible.

This is not to say that there is nothing morally objectionable about the gangster, or even about his conduct. But the negative moral assessments that are appropriate here concern the *meaning* of his action rather than its permissibility. As I argued in the preceding chapters, the meaning of an action—its significance for the agent's relations with others—depends on the agent's reasons for performing it in a way that the permissibility of the action generally does not. For example, an action that is permissible can have any one of many different meanings—may indicate quite different things about the agent's relations with others—depending on the agent's reasons for acting in that way. The agent may believe that others have rights and take them very seriously, or, like Parfit's gangster, she may think that others count for nothing but see no reason for mistreating the person in question on this particular occasion.

The injunction to "treat others as ends in themselves," like any injunction to treat certain considerations as reasons, can be understood in two ways, either as a claim about what reasons there are—in this case, a claim about permissibility—or as a directive about what attitudes to have—in this case, a claim about what an agent has to count as reasons in order for an action to have a certain kind of significance, namely to indicate the morally best kind of attitude toward others. It is not surprising that a general characterization of the distinction between right and wrong should be open to these dual interpretations. My contractualist formula, in particular, aims to explain what has to be the case for an action to be impermissible. But it aims to do this in a way that also makes clear the reasons that will move a moral person to avoid actions she sees as impermissible.

In Kant's case this duality is particularly unsurprising,

since the idea of "moral worth" is a central notion of his moral philosophy. Kant says that for an action to have moral worth it is not enough that it be "in accord with duty" (that is, permissible); it must also be "done from duty."[10] So what Kant calls moral worth is like what I am calling meaning, in its dependence on the reasons for which an action is performed. In this respect, moral worth and meaning belong to the same genus of moral assessment.

Concern with what an agent takes to be reasons may seem already involved in Kant's idea of action "in accord with duty," given that the various formulations of the categorical imperative deal with the *maxims* of actions. Since maxims have to do with reasons for acting, it may seem to follow that insofar as these formulas are conditions of permissibility, they make the permissibility of an action depend on the agent's reasons.

But there is ambiguity here of the kind I have just been discussing. An agent's maxim characterizes an action in terms of the agent's (proposed) reasons for performing it. But a maxim can also be seen as expressing a judgment (a policy) as to whether these reasons are sufficient grounds for action. So a directive to act on a certain maxim (or not to do so) can be understood in either of two ways. It can be understood as a judgment about reasons—about the correctness or incorrectness of the maxim, understood as claiming that certain reasons are adequate grounds for action—and hence as a judgment of the permissibility of so acting. Alternatively, it can be read as an assessment of the meaning of an action taken for those reasons, and a directive to perform actions only if they have certain meaning. It is natural for us to read the categorical imperative, particularly in its universal-law formulation, in the former way. Read in this way, asking whether we could will that everyone may act on a certain maxim (that is to say, that they may take certain reasons as sufficient grounds for a certain action), is a way of testing whether those reasons are sufficient. Given Kant's interest in moral worth, it is not surprising that there is another way to read his formulas, however, as a claim about the importance of acting for certain reasons, and thus as a claim about what I am calling meaning. This latter reading is perhaps more strongly suggested (although not, I would say, required) by the wording of the humanity-as-an-end and kingdom-of-ends formulations.

Although Kant's idea of moral worth has something in common with what I am calling the meaning of an action, there are important differences between the two. For Kant, to say that an action has moral worth is to say that it reflects a distinctive feature of the agent's will, which consists in that will's being responsive to duty (the moral law) without any dependence on inclination. To see how this is related to what I am calling the meaning of an action, it will help to consider some examples of the kind that Kant himself discusses.

Imagine a man who helps someone else at some cost to himself. He might do this for many different reasons. He might help the person because he likes him. Or he might help him because one of his aims in general is to help others when he can, and not just people whom he is fond of. Or he might see helping others as a duty, as something he is morally required to do, not simply as an end that he happens to have. The meaning of the man's action will be different depending on which of these reasons (or which combination of them) he takes to count in favor of acting in this way. If the person who is helped has considered this man as his friend, then the fact that the help was given for the first of these reasons (among others) gives the action a special meaning, as an expression of friendship. If, however, the supposed friend saw no reason of this kind to help, then this fact about his reasons would also give the action particular meaning, as casting doubt on the reality of the friendship, even if he did help the person for one or both of the other reasons.

If someone is in dire need, the fact that an agent sees this as giving rise to no reason of the third kind I mentioned (no moral claim for help) says something important about that agent's attitude toward others, and his relations with them. There is something lacking in those relations, for example, if a person helps others only as part of a personal quest and not at all because he sees them as entitled to aid, or sees himself as morally required to aid them. This is so even between friends. We hope that our friends will help us not merely out of duty but also because they see us as entitled to help (from them and from others) when we are in great need.

This view, that even if a person helps others out of sympathy or affection, there is something morally lacking in him if he does not see the needs of others as having any moral claim on him, might seem to express the intuitive moral idea behind Kant's doctrine that an action has moral worth only if it is done from duty. Kant is sometimes interpreted as holding that an action can have moral worth only if the motive of duty is the only factor moving the agent to act. But he need not be read so narrowly. As I argued in the previous chapter, an agent may see many considerations as providing reasons for an action, and when this is so, there may be no answer to the question of what is *the* reason for his action. Barbara Herman has suggested that when an agent sees a number of considerations as reasons, then, if the action is required by duty, we should count it as having moral worth in Kant's sense if the agent takes the fact that it is required as a conclusive reason for doing it.[11]

So Kant and I may agree that it matters whether an agent recognizes moral reasons as conclusive grounds for action, whatever other reasons he or she may also be moved by. Where our views differ is in the kind of importance that we take to be involved. In my view, the importance in question is a matter of the significance of an action for the agent's relations with others. Our relationship with a friend—what we can expect from him and the meaning of our interactions—is different if he helps us only out of affection, or only out of duty, or if he sees both reasons as relevant. Similarly, a stranger may help us at least partly because he sees that we need help and have a claim on those who can provide it, or he may do so only because he is bored and sees our predicament as posing an interesting technical challenge. The meaning of our interaction, and what it indicates about our relationship, is different depending on which of these is the case.

Kant recognizes that friendship involves being moved both by love and by respect—that is, by duty.[12] But the significance he assigns to being moved by the motive of duty is not just its significance for our relations with one another. His famous remark at the beginning of the *Groundwork*, that "there is no possibility of thinking of anything at all in the world, or even outside of it, which can be regarded as good without qualification, except a good will," suggests a more impersonal kind of value.[13] Similarly, in *Critique of Practical Reason* he says that the incentive of pure practical reason is "nothing else than the pure moral law itself, so far as it lets us perceive the sublimity of our own supersensuous existence and subjectively effects respect for their higher vocation in men who are conscious of their sensuous existence and of the accompanying dependence on their pathologically affected nature."[14] He goes on to contrast this incentive with the "charms and pleasures of life" that are associated with moral conduct, which I assume would include the kind of relations with others that I am taking to be of basic importance.

To conclude the argument of this section, the idea that we should treat all rational beings as ends in themselves is plausibly understood as a general characterization of moral permissibility. Understood in this way, however, it does not in itself make the permissibility of an action depend on what the agent saw as reasons for performing it. (It seems to do this only if we confuse its role as a general criterion of permissibility with its role as a characterization of a distinctive form of moral motivation.) But this conclusion does not rule out the possibility that, in particular cases, the permissibility of an action may depend on the agent's reasons for performing it— the possibility that, for example, some principles that could not reasonably be rejected may rule out actions that are taken for certain reasons. This is the possibility that I examined in the previous chapter and will consider further in the next section.

Treating Someone Merely as a Means

For the purposes of discussion, I will say that an action fails to treat someone as an end in himself if it fails to satisfy the formulas described in the first section of this chapter, such as my contractualist formula or one of Kant's, ignoring for the present the differences between them. One might understand "treating someone merely as a means" simply to mean not treating him as an end. But my main aim in this section will be to investigate the idea that some actions may be wrong (may fail to satisfy these formulas) *because* they involve treating someone merely as a means in some more specific sense of that phrase. What might that sense be?

The charge, "You were just using me!" does seem to identify a distinct kind of wrong. If I fail to help someone when I have a duty to do so, it does not follow that I am *using* them. The same is true if I kill someone by setting off an explosion for some other purpose or by operating my mine in such a way that the chemical runoff poisons his well. If I am treating people merely as means in these cases, it is only in the broader sense that means I am failing to treat them as ends in themselves.

So what is involved in merely using someone in the narrower sense? For me to be "merely using" a person, it might be said, I must be using them, and for this to be true their presence or participation must play a role in what I am doing. The wrongs I mentioned a moment ago (failing to aid someone, or recklessly endangering my neighbor's life) are not instances of using someone, or treating them as a means, because in those cases the ways in which the victims are involved in or affected by what I do make no difference to the accomplishment of my ends.

But the mere fact that someone's participation, or some effect on him, is essential to my achieving my aims in the way I intend (the fact that that person is a means in the ordinary sense of that word) is not sufficient to make my action morally objectionable, let alone impermissible. If it were sufficient, all cooperative activity would be impermissible. So something more must be involved in treating someone *merely* as a means, if this is to be a reason why some actions are wrong. One natural suggestion is that what is objectionable is to treat someone as a means—to pursue one's end in a way that depends on this person's presence or participation—without that person's consent. Tools can be treated that way but persons cannot—they cannot be treated as mere means.

Christine Korsgaard develops a version of this idea. She suggests that we treat a person merely as a means when we treat them in a way to which they *could not possibly* consent.[15] Understood in one way, to say that they "could not possibly consent" would mean just that they could not rationally will a principle permitting them to be treated in this way (or, in my version, that they could reasonably reject any such principle). This would simply mean that they were not being treated as ends in themselves in the sense described earlier, and it may be that this is what Korsgaard has in mind. But what we are looking for is a more specific idea of "treating someone as a means" that would explain *why* someone could not will (or could reasonably reject) a principle that would allow certain particular kinds of actions, and Korsgaard goes on to give examples that suggest a more specific objection that might play this role.

She says that we treat someone merely as a means if the maxim of our action precludes the possibility of his or her consent. The examples she gives are deception and coercion. In both of these cases an agent's plan is to circumvent a person's will—to avoid making the interaction that the agent intends depend on the person's consent, because the agent knows that the person would not give it. So it is part of the very nature of coercion and deception that the victim is put in a position that precludes the possibility of his consenting, or effectively refusing to consent, to what the agent is doing. This does seem to capture a powerful objection to certain forms of action. As I would put it, we can have good reason to object to having our will subverted in this way, and this explains why principles permitting this kind of conduct could reasonably be rejected.[16] But there are several problems with this idea.

One problem is that not all plans of action that depend on the impossibility of a person's giving or withholding consent are wrong. There is such a thing as permissible deception and even, I would say, permissible coercion. The most plausible cases of permissible coercion either involve wrongdoing or the threat of wrongdoing on the part of the person coerced or else are cases in which this person has severely diminished rational capacities (such as a case in which it is permissible to forcibly restrain someone who is having a psychotic episode). These might be classed as special cases in which normal prohibitions are set aside. The same might be argued for cases of permissible deception, and it might therefore be said that coercion and deception are permissible only in these abnormal cases.[17]

It seems to me, however, that there are cases that are clearly within the scope of normal morality in which the kind of "subversion of the will" that is involved in Korsgaard's examples is not wrong. Suppose, for example, that A is going to attend a conference in Paris. He knows that if B were to learn that he was going, then B would go to the conference too (something she has every right to do). Since B's presence would lead to A's having a much less enjoyable and successful trip, A takes care not to tell B that he is going. He does not do this by lying to B but only by being careful not to say or do anything that would lead to B's learning of his trip. Whether this counts as a case of deception or not, it is clearly a case in which the subversion of B's will is an essential part of A's plan. A knows that if B were aware of his trip she would go as well. So A takes care not to give B the chance to do that.

It seems to me that what A does in this example need not be wrong. Whether it is or not depends on whether B has any claim to be informed of A's plans. I have not said anything about what the relation between them is. For all I have said, B might be an ex-spouse or a would-be lover of A, or an annoying colleague at another university, who always asks extremely long and boring questions. In cases like these A would not wrong B by concealing his plans, because B has no claim on A that he let B know what he is doing. And in order for B to have no claim, she need not have done A any wrong, nor have threatened to do so.

The wrong that we are considering here—the one

brought to mind by Korsgaard's examples—occurs when the following is true:

1. A's action affects or involves B in a way that is impermissible unless B consents to it.
2. Under the circumstances, B lacks the opportunity to give or withhold consent.

This wrong is made more evident when it is also true that

3. Given proper opportunity, B would refuse to consent to what A does.

Let us call this wrong *costly involvement without consent.* The consent in question here is obviously *actual* consent. We might, of course, answer the question of when actual consent is required by asking whether B could rationally will a principle permitting A to act without her actual consent in such a case (or whether B could reasonably reject such a principle). And if the answer is that B could not, then we might say that what A does in such a case is wrong "because B could not possibly consent to it." But I hope it is clear that we would here be appealing to an idea of hypothetical consent that is part of a general characterization of right and wrong, rather than the kind of actual consent that is at issue in the particular class of wrongs we are considering—the kind that deception or coercion can render a victim unable to give.

My formulation of this wrong is very broad. It leaves it open whether, as in the cases of coercion and deception that Korsgaard discusses, A brings it about that B lacks proper opportunity to give or withhold consent or whether, as in what might be called exploitation cases, A just takes advantage of B's lack of information or unfortunate circumstances. Even more broadly, the wrong as I have described it can occur when it is no part of A's *plan* that B will be unable to consent, or refuse to consent, to what A does. Suppose A and B are adjacent landowners who share rights to the water in a stream that flows across their fields. If A diverts the water without B's consent, then he commits the wrong I have described whether he does it by stealth (at night, so that B will not notice in time) or by coercing B into giving his consent, or he simply does it heedlessly, having given no thought at all to B's rights in the matter. These actions have different meanings—one's relations with one's neighbor are altered in different ways by being tricked, being threatened, or having one's rights simply ignored—but these differences are not relevant to the permissibility of what is done. All of these actions are impermissible because they are instances of the wrong I have defined.

My definition of wrongful costly involvement without consent makes no reference to the idea of treating someone as a means. It says only that A's action "affects or involves B." This would seem to include cases, such as the case of failing to save a drowning person, in which B is not a means to any end of A's. I defined the wrong in this broad way because I wanted, as a first step, to identify the class of cases in which what makes something wrong is the lack, or impossibility, of consent. If the idea of a means plays a role here, it must be because "being a means" is *one* form of involvement in an agent's action that can trigger a requirement of consent.

What, then, has to be the case in order for B to be involved in A's action as a means? To begin with, the action must involve some cost to B and some benefit to A. But these conditions are fulfilled in the stream case, in which it does not seem that B is a means, and even in the drowning case, in which this is even clearer. In order for B to be a means, the way in which he or she is involved or affected must be part of what produces the benefit to A. In the stream case, although the divergence of the water away from B's land is essential to the benefit to A, the impact that this has on B is immaterial. In the Paris case, by contrast, it is *B's not being in Paris* that benefits A, and this makes it more plausible to say in that case that B is treated as a means. It is even more plausible to say this in a case that involves some positive intentional action on B's part. Suppose, to change the example, that A wants B to attend the conference in Paris, because he wants B to attend his lecture. B, on the other hand, thinks it is worth going only because she believes, falsely, that she will have the chance to meet C, a French intellectual who is one of her heroes. A knows that C will not be there, but fails to tell B, because he wants B to make the trip.

This change in the example makes it clear that what A does to B is wrong, and makes it more plausible to say that he has treated B as a means. The change makes the wrong more obvious because it makes it clear that B is entitled to make an informed decision about whether to go or not, and that A has an obligation to reveal information he knows to be relevant to this decision. It may also be true that B's going to Paris advances A's ends, and is thus a means, but this fact in itself plays no role in explaining why what A does is wrong. That is sufficiently explained by the factors I have already mentioned.

In other cases, however, the fact that B's participation will advance A's ends can have greater significance. Consider a different example, in which A and B are both planning to attend the conference, and A wants B, who is an important person in the field, to go to the conference with him and to attend the lecture he will be giving there. What he does not tell B is that he wants this because D, who is considering A for a possible appointment, will take B's presence as a sign that she respects A and thinks well of his work. In this case A is treating B as a means ("using" her) and what he does is probably wrong. The wrong in question, however, is that A wrongfully deprives B of information she needs to make an informed decision about whether to go to the conference and attend the lecture. The idea of a means comes in, at a less fundamental level, as part of the explanation of why this information is important.

It can do this in two ways. First, it might be that B does not want A to get the job and would not attend his lecture if she thought that it would make this more likely. Second, even if B is indifferent as to whether A gets the job or not, she may not want to contribute toward his getting it. Perhaps B is friends both with A and with E, who is under consideration for the same job. She would be happy to see either of them get the job but does not want to do anything that would be instrumental in aiding one of them over the other. The first of these considerations concerns B's preferences about the possible outcome of her action; the second concerns the meaning of her action—the significance of her doing something that would aid A, whether or not A got the job.

The general point is that we have reason to care about what ends we will be promoting in choosing a certain action, and therefore reason to want to know what those ends are before deciding how to act.[18] So, in contrast to earlier cases in which the idea of a means played no role in explaining the wrongfulness of A's action, here the fact that B will be involved as a means to A's end can be relevant to whether A's treatment of B is wrong.

We should notice, however, that the reasons B has for wanting to know what end she will be promoting by attending A's lecture need not depend on the fact that this is an end *of A's*. This can be brought out by considering a slightly different example. Suppose that A and B are attending the annual meeting of their professional association, at which A will be speaking. A would like B to attend his lecture simply because B is a friend. But A knows that the executive committee of the association has decided that it must reduce the number of sessions devoted to various subfields, and that committee members will be visiting some sessions, including the one at which A is speaking, in order to decide which ones to discontinue. Since B is a prominent member of the profession, her attendance at the session will help make it appear to be an important and active subfield. Although A knows all this, he does not care which sessions get eliminated. But B, who has no idea that this is going on, may care. She may think that if some sessions are going to be eliminated it would be better to drop the sessions of the kind at which A is speaking, and so she would rather not contribute to the case for keeping these sessions. Or it could be that B is indifferent as to which sessions are dropped but wishes to remain neutral on the question, and to avoid doing anything to favor the continuance of any one session, because she has good friends in several of the subfields that might be affected. So B has reasons, of the same kinds as in the previous example, to want to be informed about the ends she will be serving if she attends the lecture. If feelings are running strong about which subfield's sessions should be eliminated, those reasons could be quite compelling.

What this brings out is that the wrong involved in both examples is a failure to inform, rather than treating someone as a means to one's ends. Even if the wrong in both cases is the same, however, the interactions between A and B in the two cases have a different meaning: in the former case, but not the latter, A is "using" B. I will explore the significance of this difference in the next section.

"Using" and Meaning

The idea that participating in a certain action would involve "being used" can itself figure as something that a person has good reason to want to be informed of before deciding whether to participate. To see how this might be the case, we must return to the idea of the meaning of an action, and to the question of how the permissibility of an action can depend on the agent's reasons for performing it. I will consider a case of very personal interaction, where the importance of meaning may be clearest. But I believe that the point applies to less personal interactions as well.

Suppose you invite me to the big end-of-the-year dance. The meaning of going to the dance with you depends on your reasons for inviting me. It is one thing if you are expressing a romantic interest in me, another if you are proposing that we go "just as friends" because that would be more fun than staying home. It would be something still different if your aim were to annoy your former lover, or to have a chance to associate with the "in crowd," which accepts me as a member. I might be willing to go with you if you have some of these reasons in mind but not if you are moved only by others. Suppose I accept your invitation thinking that it expresses your interest in me, either as lover or friend. If I then find out that this was not true, that your concerns were only of some of the other kinds just listed, then I might say, in anger, "You were just using me!" In saying this I might be protesting that it was wrong of you to get me to go with you on false pretenses. But I might also be making a claim about your reasons for inviting me (the reasons you were concealing). I had assumed that you were guided by a certain kind of concern for me, but it turned out that this was not so at all. You were "just using me"—that is to say, you were taking me to the dance because this served purposes for you that had nothing to do with any concern for me. This fact about your reasons changes the meaning of our going together. I might well object to being invited for those reasons even if no deception at all were involved (and this may be what makes the deception necessary).

But the fact that you were "just using" me in this sense need not, by itself, make your action wrong. We would not wrong each other by going to the dance together with the shared understanding that we were each doing so only for the sake of other aims. (Although one of us might regret the fact that we had no more interest in each other than this.) It can be wrong to get someone to go with you by deceiving him or her about the meaning of this interaction, and an action can be a wrong of this type even if it does not involve using a person in the sense I have just been describing. For example, because dancing with you has a particular meaning if you have a romantic interest in me, I may be willing to go to the dance with you only if your interest is not of a romantic nature. It might therefore be wrong for you to get me to go with you by concealing the fact that you are hopelessly in love with me. But in such a case the charge that you are "just using me" would not have the same force as in the cases described above.[19] "Just using" in the sense I am describing here is thus one kind of meaning that an interaction can have, and one kind of meaning that it can be wrong to deceive someone about. But it is not the only kind.

Conclusion

My aim in this chapter has been to explain the apparent moral significance of the ideas of treating someone as an end and treating someone merely as a means. I have tried to do this with the help of two distinctions. The first is between, on the one hand, a general characterization of the distinction between right and wrong, and, on the other, an account of what makes a certain class of actions wrong. I suggested that the requirement that we treat others as ends in themselves offers a plausible general characterization of the distinction between right and wrong. In contrast, I argued that there are more specific ideas of "treating someone as a means" and "using someone" that play a role in explaining why certain particular actions are wrong, although they do not play a fundamental role in these explanations.

My second distinction was between the permissibility of an action and its meaning. Understood in one way, the idea of treating others as ends in themselves is a very abstract account of permissibility. But the idea that we must *treat* others as ends in themselves can also be understood as a claim about the attitude we must have in order for our actions to have a certain kind of meaning—namely, for them to express an important kind of respect for others. Understood in the latter way, whether an action involves treating a person as an end in himself depends on what the agent saw as reasons; understood in the former way, as a condition of permissibility, it does not.

The more specific charge of "just using" someone has a similar ambiguity. It can be used to refer to a particular species of wrong, or to an attitude that can affect the meaning of an action. These two can be related. The fact that our interaction has a certain meaning can be part of what makes it wrong. But the two ideas are independent of each other. An action can be wrong for reasons that are independent of its meaning.

Taken altogether, these points seem to me to explain the various ways in which the ideas of treating someone as an end and treating someone merely as a means can be significant. No doubt there are other loose threads that I have not picked up, but the account I have given seems to me to explain most of them. I will close by emphasizing one kind of significance that the idea of a means does not have, in my view.

According to the view I have outlined, the fact that a person's presence, or his or her action, is causally necessary for another person's plan may indicate that the plan involves this person in a way that requires his or her consent. But being a means in this sense—being causally necessary—has no intrinsic moral significance, in my view. What matters is the cost to the person of being involved, and the claim that person has to be informed about the nature of this involvement.

This analysis has some implications for the possibility of using the idea of being treated as a means to explain why it is permissible to switch a runaway train that is headed for five people onto a sidetrack where only one person will be hit, but not permissible to throw one person off of a bridge in order to stop the train. It is true that in the bridge case, the one person's being thrown from the bridge and thus hit by the train is necessary to the agent's plan, and this involvement is costly to that person: he will almost certainly be killed. In the simple trolley case it is not necessary, in order to save five, that the single person on the sidetrack be hit. But it remains true that that person will be hit, and this involvement is costly: he, too, will almost certainly die.

Assuming that in the simple trolley case it is permissible to turn the trolley, inflicting this cost on the one without his consent, the question is whether the fact that the person's death is causally necessary to save the five in the bridge example makes it the case that his consent is required. Based on the analysis I have offered, this depends on the claim that the person has to be informed about the end he is serving. The person might care about this. He might, for example, particularly hate the five whose lives are in danger and not wish to contribute to saving their lives. But the fact that he might have such reasons does not seem to make it the case that his consent is required. If it did, why should consent not also be required in the simple trolley case, since the single person on the sidetrack might have the same reasons not to want to be sacrificed to save the five. The fact that his involvement is not causally necessary does not seem to make a significant difference. The difference in meaning might be greater if the bridge case involved some positive intentional action on the part of the one. But in being thrown from the bridge, the person in that case is just as passive as the person on the track who is hit by the train. Thus if there is a difference in meaning between the two cases, it is too slight to ground a requirement of consent that would account for the difference in permissibility.

The same analysis applies to Thomson's version of the trolley problem in which the branch line loops around and rejoins the main line in the opposite direction. In this example, switching the train onto the sidetrack where one person is standing saves the others only because the train will be stopped by hitting the one. Here again the question is whether the fact that the involvement of the one person is causally necessary to save the five gives rise to a requirement of consent that is not present in the simple trolley case. For the reasons I have given, the answer seems to me that it does not.

So the idea of treating someone as a means cannot explain the difference between switching the train and throwing the person from the bridge unless this idea has greater moral significance than I have been able to find for it. Perhaps the difference between these cases lies, as Thomson has suggested, in a difference in what is done to the individuals that puts them in harm's way.[20] If what would be done in the bridge case is impermissible, this may be because we have a claim against others not to be thrown off bridges, and the need to save five others does not justify an exception to this claim. But our claim not to have dangerous threats directed toward us may admit of such an exception: it may be permissible to redirect existing threats so that they threaten fewer people. I am not

certain that this is the proper explanation. But it seems unlikely to me that the proper explanation of the difference between these cases, whatever it may be, turns on the idea that in
one case, but not in the other, the effect on the one person is a
means to saving the others.

4

Blame

In this chapter I offer an account of blame, based on the distinction between permissibility and meaning presented in the preceding chapters. Blame is a familiar aspect of moral experience, but it is surprisingly unclear exactly what it involves. Accounts of blame tend toward two ideas. The first idea is essentially evaluative: that to blame someone is to arrive at a negative assessment of his or her character. The second is punitive: blame is a kind of sanction, a milder form of punishment. Neither of these interpretations seems to me to fit the facts of our moral experience. The alternative account presented in this chapter seems to me to be a better fit, although it also has aspects that will no doubt strike some as revisionist.

On the interpretation I offer, blame normally involves more than an evaluation but is not a kind of sanction. To blame a person for an action, in my view, is to take that action to indicate something about the person that impairs one's relationship with him or her, and to understand that relationship in a way that reflects this impairment. This account seems to me to fit with much of what we say about blame, and with the significance it has for us. It also explains various facts about what I call the ethics of blame: about who can be blamed, who has standing to blame, and why we should blame—why blame is not an attitude we would do better to avoid.

Questions about the nature of blame lie behind the philosophical controversies about freedom and responsibility. Many believe that moral blame is appropriate only for actions or characteristics that are under an agent's control, and some maintain that agents have control in the relevant sense only if their actions and characteristics are not due to things outside of them, such as their genetic makeup, their social circumstances, and other environmental factors. But it is not commonly explained why this should be so. Whether blame requires freedom, and what kind of freedom or control it requires, surely depends on what blame is. If, for example, blame is merely a kind of negative evaluation, then it is not clear why control or freedom should be required. I will identify what seem to me to be the strongest reasons for thinking that blame presupposes a strong kind of freedom, and explain why these do not apply to blame when it is understood in the way I propose.

What Is Blame?

In most cases, to decide that what a person has done is blameworthy is in part to decide that he has behaved wrongly—that he has acted in a way that is contrary to standards that we all have reason to regard as important and normally overriding. These can't be just any standards. Failing to meet the standards of athletic or artistic performance, or making mistakes in arithmetic, are not in themselves grounds for blame. Such standards do not have the right kind of importance, and their violation does not, in itself, have the right kind of significance to make blame appropriate.

It is not easy to say exactly what kind of importance standards have to have in order to be *moral* standards. I doubt whether there is a single, more substantive account of distinctively moral importance that covers all the cases people commonly refer to as "moral."[1] But I believe that, at least in a large and central class of cases, distinctively moral standards have to do with the kind of concern that we owe to each other. The importance of moral standards, at least in these cases, thus lies in the importance for us of our relations with other people. I will concentrate on the kind of blame that is associated with wrongness of this kind, generally leaving aside interesting questions about blame for violating other kinds of standards that may be called moral.

When someone is blameworthy, it is generally for doing something that was wrong. But wrongness and blame can come apart. The blameworthiness of an action depends, in ways that wrongness generally does not, on the reasons for which a person acted and the conditions under which he or she did so. So it can be appropriate to say such things as, "Yes, what she did was certainly wrong, but you shouldn't blame her. She was under great stress," or "You can't blame him. He thought he was acting for the best." Good intentions, and conditions such as stress, can be relevant to blame even when they are not relevant to the rightness or wrongness of what the person did. It can also make sense to blame a person even when what he did was not impermissible. For example, it can be appropriate to blame a person who has done what was in fact the right thing if he or she did it for an extremely bad reason.

Something *similar* to blame may also apply to people who, for perfectly good reasons, do something that turns out very badly for others. A political leader, for example, may choose what there is good reason to think is the best action, but it may nonetheless have disastrous consequences. If it does, then she may find it difficult to live with herself, and others, too, may regard her as a pariah if, for instance, her choice led to the death of thousands. The same is true in more personal cases, as in an example offered by Thomas Nagel. A person who, while doing something he has every reason to believe is quite safe—driving down his street—kills his own child or a neighbor's child through a freak accident, may understandably find it difficult to live with the fact that he is the one who killed her. As Nagel observes, this is not a case of moral blame.[2] It is quite natural to reassure such a person by saying that he is blameless. Nonetheless, what such a person is likely to suffer seems somehow akin to blame, in a way that needs to be explained.

Nagel distinguishes this phenomenon, which might be called objective stigma, from cases of genuine moral luck. He writes:

> However, if the driver was guilty of even a minor degree of negligence—failing to have his brakes checked

recently, for example—then if that negligence contributes to the death of the child, he will not merely feel
terrible. He will blame himself for the death. And what
makes this an example of moral luck is that he would
have to blame himself only slightly for the negligence if
no situation arose which required him to brake suddenly
and violently to avoid hitting a child. Yet the *negligence*
is the same in both cases, and the driver has no control
over whether a child will run into his path.[3]

I will refer to cases in which blame appears to vary in this way
as instances of moral outcome luck. An adequate account of
blame should either explain how blame can vary in the way
that these examples suggest or else give a convincing explanation of why it should appear to do so even though it does not.

If wrongness and blameworthiness can diverge in these
ways, what does a judgment of blameworthiness amount to? It
might be said that to blame someone for something is to count
it (negatively) as part of his "moral record."[4] But what is this
record and what are we doing in keeping it? Is it just a record
of what the person did that was wrong? If so, how could what
he did be wrong but *not* be part of his record?

It is also natural to say that blaming someone is a matter
of assessing his or her character, whereas wrongness has to
do only with the action he or she performed. There is clearly
something right about this. But although blaming may have to
do with character, it also has to do with an action—at least in
many cases we blame a person *for* something. So it might be
said that to blame a person for something is to take that action
as showing something negative about that person's character.[5]

This has the advantage of explaining why blame should depend on the agent's reasons for performing an action, and on the conditions (such as great stress) under which an action is performed, since both of these are relevant to the question of what one can infer from an action about the character of the agent.

By itself, however, this view does not explain the distinctive weight that moral blame seems to have. Unless we say more about why we are interested in this kind of character assessment, it may seem to be a pointless assignment of moral "grades." Our interest in people's character might, of course, be prudential. We have an obvious interest in deciding whom we can rely on, for example. But this does not capture all that blame involves. It is not unreasonable to continue to blame someone for an action even when we are quite certain that the opportunity to display the relevant kind of character flaw is unlikely ever to recur.

Moreover, the "character assessment" account of blame, by itself, leaves us with no way to explain the phenomenon of moral outcome luck. The driver in Nagel's example has exactly the same character—has shown the same degree of carelessness—if a child runs out in front of him or if one does not. So if there is any difference in the blame that is appropriate in the two cases, blame must involve something other than the assessment of character.

One alternative view, suggested by Peter Strawson, identifies blame with reactive attitudes such as resentment and indignation.[6] An account of this kind has several advantages over one that understands blame in terms of disapproval or character assessment. First, and most important, it avoids the charge that blame involves a pointless assignment of moral grades. As Strawson says, it is an essential component of normal interpersonal relations that we should be susceptible to feeling indignation and resentment toward those who, we believe, fail to show the kind of concern for others that these relationships demand. Second, this account can allow for the ways in which the content of blame varies. Different relationships involve different standards. (In Strawson's terms, they demand different forms of "good will.") And different reactions are appropriate, depending on one's relation to the person who fails to show the concern demanded by these standards.

But this view, by itself, still fails to explain the plausibility of moral outcome luck. If the reactive attitudes that blame involves are reactions to the *attitudes* of others as manifested in their conduct—for example to the concern for the interests of others that their actions manifest—then moral outcome luck still seems inexplicable.

The account of blame that I offer is like Strawson's in seeing human relationships as the foundations of blame. But it differs from his view in placing emphasis on the expectations, intentions, and other attitudes that constitute these relationships rather than on moral emotions such as resentment and indignation. Briefly put, my proposal is this: to claim that a person is *blameworthy* for an action is to claim that the action shows something about the agent's attitudes toward others that impairs the relations that others can have with him or her.[7] To *blame* a person is to judge him or her to be blameworthy and to take your relationship with him or her to be modified in a way that this judgment of impaired relations holds to be appropriate. To understand this proposal, it will help to begin with an analogy between impersonal morality and more personal relationships, such as those that hold between good friends or lovers.

Suppose I learn that at a party last week some acquaintances were talking about me, and making some cruel jokes at my expense. I further learn that my close friend Joe was at the party, and that rather than coming to my defense or adopting a stony silence, he was laughing heartily and even contributed a few barbs, revealing some embarrassing facts about me that I had told him in confidence. This raises a question about my relationship with Joe. Should I still consider Joe to be my friend? This is not just a question about his future conduct. It may be that circumstances like those prevailing at the party—the particular combustible mix of personal and chemical influences—is very unlikely ever to recur. And it may be that Joe feels very bad about the way he behaved and that this also indicates that his conduct is unlikely to be repeated. The question is not just about how he will act in the future but about what happened in the past, and what it indicates about Joe's attitude toward me and about the nature of our relationship.

Possible responses, on my part, to what Joe has done fall into three general categories. First, I might consider whether I should continue to regard Joe as a friend. An answer to this question is a judgment about the meaning of Joe's action—about what it shows about his attitude toward me, considered in relation to the requirements of friendship, and about the significance of that attitude for our relationship. Second, I might revise my attitude toward Joe in the way that this judgment holds to be appropriate. I might, for example, cease to value spending time with him in the way one does with a friend, and I might revise my intentions to confide in him and to encourage him to confide in me. Third, I might complain to Joe about his conduct, demand an explanation or justification, or indicate in some other way that I no longer see him as a friend.[8]

These three forms of response are closely linked, but there is a degree of independence between them. Insofar as one's relations with a person are constituted by the reasons one takes oneself to have for treating him or her in certain ways, a judgment of blameworthiness, taken seriously, marks a change in that relationship and hence is a form of blame. When one has made such a judgment, however, there remains the question of how seriously one is going to take it, and how far one is going to go in adjusting one's attitude toward the person in the ways that this judgment claims are appropriate. I might reach the conclusion that Joe's conduct makes it inappropriate to go on thinking of him as a friend but nonetheless continue to treat him as one in the ways just mentioned. This might be irrational or self-deceptive, since it would involve a failure to hold to the attitude I myself judge to be appropriate. It might also indicate a kind of weakness or servility on my part. I may be dependent on Joe and crave his attention to a degree that leads me to behave in a demeaning manner. Even if I decide that Joe is not really a good friend and revise my attitude toward him accordingly, however, it is a further question whether I will express this to Joe, and in what way. Self-respect may require that I speak up for myself, rather than merely walking away from our relationship in silence.

To understand blame in general it is important to distinguish between responses of the three kinds I have listed and, in particular, not to simply identify blame with a response of the third kind. The conclusion that someone is blameworthy for something he or she has done is a response of the first kind: a judgment that the action shows that person to hold attitudes that impair his or her relations with others. To blame the person is to hold the attitude toward him or her that this impairment makes appropriate. In the examples I have discussed, blaming someone involves *revising* one's attitude toward him or her. But blameworthy conduct can also simply confirm the negative conclusion we have already reached about a person's attitudes toward us and others, in which case to blame is just to reaffirm the attitudes that this judgment holds to be appropriate.[9] The attitudes blame involves may include intentions to complain to the person, and to demand an explanation, justification, or apology, but these need not be present in every instance of blaming.

To explain and defend this account of blame, I need to say more about the ideas of a relationship, the impairment of a relationship, and the responses that this impairment can make appropriate.

Personal Relationships and Impairment

A relationship is constituted by certain attitudes and dispositions. Central among these are intentions and expectations about how the parties will act toward one another. But relationships also include intentions and expectations about the feelings that the parties have for one another, and the considerations that they are disposed to respond to and see as reasons.

The variety of attitudes that relationships involve is clear in the case of friendship. To be friends with a person involves such things as intending to give help and support when needed, beyond what one would be obligated to do for just anyone; intending to confide in the person and to keep his or her confidences in return; and intending to spend time with the person when one can, and to "keep in touch." Being a friend involves actually being disposed to act in these ways, not just having an abstract intention to do so. It also involves being disposed to do these things for the right kinds of reasons, not only out of a sense of obligation but also out of a certain kind of concern and affection for each other.[10]

In addition to these intentions and dispositions to behave in certain ways (to fulfill what might be called the obligations of friendship), being a friend involves being disposed to certain feelings: to take pleasure in the friend's company, to hope that things go well for the friend and to take pleasure in their going well when they do. A friend is not *obligated* to have such hopes and feelings, but a person who fails to have them, if a friend at all, is a deficient one.

If a friend is under consideration for a good job, or has bought a lottery ticket, it would be disloyal not to hope that they get the job or win the prize (leaving aside the possibility of conflicting loyalties). To hope that these things will happen, or even to see oneself, as a friend, as having reason to hope that they will happen, need not involve believing that there is more reason for one's friend to get the job, or win the prize, than for someone else to do so. One has reason to hope for these things simply because the person is one's friend, but these reasons need not be based on what one judges to be objectively best overall.

In a true friendship the attitudes just described are mutual. Mutuality is not a further, independent feature of friendship but is presupposed by the attitudes that constitute it. You are disposed to confide in a friend because you suppose that he or she is disposed to keep those confidences, and also, at least as important, because you suppose that the friend cares about you and about how your life is going. Similarly, the particular kind of pleasure that you take in being with a friend presupposes that he or she takes pleasure in the interactions as well. If this is not so—if the other person is bored, or merely indulging you—then the whole thing is founded on a mistake. This is true not only of friendship but of less significant relationships as well, such as with the person from whom you regularly buy your vegetables, who always asks about your children and commiserates about the difficulties of parenthood. If this person is moved merely by the desire to keep his customers coming back, or if he would shoot you if he had any reason to, then you are making a mistake in the kind of pleasure you take in these interchanges. To put this in terms I have used earlier: the meaning of the interactions between the parties is an important aspect of personal relationships. The quality of these relationships thus depends on the reasons for which the parties are disposed to act and expect each other to act.

It is important to distinguish, here, between the normative ideal of a relationship of a certain kind, such as friendship, and particular relationships of that kind, which hold between particular individuals.[11] The normative ideal of a particular kind of relationship specifies what must be true in order for individuals to have a relationship of this kind, and specifies how individuals in such a relationship should, ideally, behave toward each other, and the attitudes that they should have. It thus sets the standards relative to which particular relationships of this kind exist and the (higher) standards relative to which such relationships can be better or worse, and can be seen as impaired.

Most personal relationships are contingent and conditional in various ways. Our relationships with neighbors, co-workers, and the tradespeople we deal with are obviously conditional on the contingent fact that we regularly interact in these ways. The same is true, in a less contingent way, of the relations between parents and children. But as the case of friendship shows, relationships can also be conditional on the attitudes of the parties involved. Friendship depends on the parties' intentions and expectations but also on the fact that they take pleasure in each other's company and have things in common, such as enjoying some of the same pursuits or having shared memories that are important to them (important both on their own and because they are shared).

Relationships that are conditional in these ways can come to an end without either party's being at fault. Friends can grow apart without either of them having been in any way disloyal or a "bad friend." They may just change, become interested in different things, and cease to value being together. These changes may bring a friendship to an end, but not in a way that is analogous to blame. A friendship might also be said to be "impaired" when one party is hit on the head and becomes comatose, or loses his memory. Such cases may call for some revision in the parties' expectations and intentions. But a judgment that a friendship has been impaired in this way is not in itself a judgment of blameworthiness, or analogous to one.

These two cases ("drifting apart" and physical injury) differ in ways that bring out the way in which they both differ from impairment of the kind I am concerned with. The people who have drifted apart may thereby cease to be friends, but physical injury does not, or should not, bring friendship to an end. The difference between the cases follows from the standards governing the attitudes that friendship involves. These standards must allow for friendships to end blamelessly. Friendship would be an oppressive relationship if it had to last forever, no matter what. But insofar as friendship involves having special concern for each other, the standards of friendship also require one to provide support and understanding when a friend is injured, rather than writing off that friend as "no fun anymore."

Assuming that the friend of the injured person remains loyal, neither the way in which a friendship is impaired by such an injury nor the way in which a friendship ends when the parties drift apart involves violation of the standards of friendship, and this is what differentiates these cases from the kind of impairment I am concerned with. Impairment of the kind I refer to occurs when one party, while standing in the relevant relation to another person, holds attitudes toward that person that are ruled out by the standards of that relationship, thus making it appropriate for the other party to have attitudes other than those that the relationship normally involves.

This could be what happens in the example of my friend

Joe's behavior at the party. At the extreme, I might conclude that Joe was not really a friend after all.[12] To conclude that this is so would be to conclude that I have reason to revise my expectations and intentions in certain ways: to decide not to rely on or confide in Joe as one would in the case of a friend, and not to seek his company, to find it reassuring, or to have the special concern for his feelings and well-being that one has for a friend's. To revise my intentions and expectations with regard to Joe in this way, or in some less extreme way, is to blame him. I might also resent his behavior, or feel some other moral emotion. But this is not required for blame, in my view—I might just feel sad.

However, the conclusion need not be this radical. If other aspects of the friendship remain intact, then the relationship can continue in an impaired form. If it does, there may be changes in the ways that the injured party has reason to behave. For example, if I have been making fun of you behind your back, then you have reason to be less free in revealing yourself to me than you would normally be with a friend. Or the shift may be purely one of attitude: you have reason to see my professions of concern for you in a different light—not, perhaps, as entirely disingenuous, but as nonetheless to be taken with more qualification than before.

I have been concentrating so far on the point of view of a person whose relationship with another is impaired by that other party's deficient attitudes, and I have been considering the attitudes and intentions that this impairment makes appropriate for a person in that position. But we should also consider the responses that are appropriate for a third party who is not a participant in the relationship. Like the injured friend, a third party can *disapprove* of the guilty party, and judge that he or she is not a good friend. But this deficiency has a different meaning for parties in these two positions.

Because the injured party is a participant in the friendship, its impairment has special significance for him. It raises questions about the meaning of his (past and future) interactions with his friend and about his responses on those occasions. Such questions do not have the same significance for a third party. This difference can be brought out by considering the idea of betrayal. The judgment that you were betrayed by your friend—a judgment that what he did was an instance of a certain kind of wrong—is one that either you or a third party can be in a position to make. But taking seriously the fact that one has been betrayed involves more than making this judgment, and more than making this judgment plus feeling a certain emotion (a special kind of resentment, perhaps). It involves seeing one's relationship with the person as changed and one's interactions with the person as having different meaning, seeing oneself as having different reasons governing those interactions and having the intention to be guided by those reasons. A third party can judge that the action of betrayal has this meaning for you, but because he is not a participant in the relationship to begin with, he is not in a position to adjust his attitudes toward the guilty party in the relevant way. Not being a friend, he cannot have the attitudes—the revised expectations, intentions, and assignments of meaning—that a wounded friend properly has.

This discussion of friendship and blame has brought out

five elements that are central to the general account of blame that I am offering:

1. The *ground relationship* (in this case friendship), which provides the standards relative to which the attitudes that an agent's action reveals constitute an impairment. These standards also determine the appropriateness of various responses to this impairment.
2. The *impairment* of a particular relationship by certain attitudes of one of the parties.
3. The *position of the responder* (the person doing the blaming) relative to the agent and the impairment. The responder might, for example, be a friend who was betrayed, a friend of that friend, or a disinterested third party.
4. The *significance of the impairment for the responder.* This is a function of the impairment and of the responder's relation to the agent, action, and impairment.
5. The *response* (blame) that is appropriate. This depends on the impairment and its significance for the responder, given his or her position. It is determined by the standards involved in the ground relationship. In the examples discussed, this response involves *revising* one's attitude toward a person.

In the case of friendship it is relatively clear what the ground relationship is. But in the general moral case, it is not so clear what relationship we are talking about when we say that to blame a person is to conclude that his relations with others are impaired. Do we have a relationship with every total stranger whom it makes sense to blame?[13] My answer is that in a general sense we do. But this requires further explanation.

The Moral Relationship

The idea that we have a relationship with everyone in the world sounds odd for at least two reasons. The first is that we naturally take the term 'relationship' to refer to a *particular* relationship, like the friendship between two individuals, which is constituted by the friends' special attitudes toward each other. Morality is not a relationship in this sense. Rather, it is a normative ideal, like a normative ideal of friendship that specifies attitudes and expectations that we should have regarding one another whenever certain conditions are fulfilled.

In the case of friendship and most other personal relations, these conditions involve the parties' attitudes toward one another, and it is in virtue of these attitudes that their relationship exists—that they are friends. In the case of morality, however, the relevant conditions do not concern the parties' existing attitudes toward one another but only certain general facts about them, namely that they are beings of a kind that are capable of understanding and responding to reasons. Insofar as one assumes that any relationship must, like friendship, be constituted by the parties' attitudes, this provides a second reason for thinking it inappropriate to say that morality defines a relationship that holds even between total strangers. But this assumption is mistaken. The conditions in virtue of which relationships exist, and the relevant normative standards therefore apply, do not always involve the parties' attitudes toward one another.

The relationship of parents to their children is a leading example: normative standards requiring care and concern for one's children apply simply in virtue of the fact that they are one's children, and depend on one for their care. Similarly, in my view, morality requires that we hold certain attitudes toward one another simply in virtue of the fact that we stand in the relation of "fellow rational beings." It requires us to take care not to behave in ways that will harm those to whom we stand in this relation, to help them when we can easily do so, not to lie to them or mislead them, and so on. A morally good person will have standing intentions to regulate his or her behavior in these ways. These intentions concern our behavior toward people in general, not simply toward specific individuals whom we are aware of or could specify. They concern behavior toward people, whoever they may be, whom we happen to interact with in various ways, such as people who may be injured by our driving, or who ask us for directions, or who need our help in other ways.

Beyond these intentions, good moral relations with others involve being disposed to have certain other attitudes. These include, in general, being disposed to be pleased when we hear of things going well for other people. We are not morally obligated to have these feelings, just as we are not obligated to be pleased when things go well for a friend. But one is deficient as a friend if one does not have such feelings, and it is a moral deficiency to hope that things go badly for others, even strangers, or to be pleased when they do.

These attitudes and dispositions define what I am calling the moral relationship: the kind of mutual concern that, ideally, we all have toward other rational beings. Calling this a relationship may seem implausible because the attitudes that make it up are so abstract—directed toward people in general, rather than toward specified individuals. It may seem to make no sense to speak of our having attitudes toward people we have no knowledge of, or about what their attitudes may be toward us, of whom they are similarly unaware. But when we do become aware of others and are in actual or potential inter-action with them, we generally assume that even if they are strangers they will manifest at least the basic elements of this ideal concern. We assume that this default relationship of mu-tual regard and forbearance holds between us and the strang-ers we pass on the road or interact with in the market. When someone does not manifest this concern, it is this relationship that is the standard relative to which our actual relation with them is seen as impaired.

To judge individuals to be blameworthy, I am claiming, is to judge that their conduct shows something about them that indicates this kind of impairment of their relations with oth-ers, an impairment that makes it appropriate for others to have attitudes toward them different from those that constitute the default moral relationship. To blame someone is actually to hold modified attitudes of this kind toward him or her.[14]

It is relatively easy to say what this type of impairment consists in. It occurs when a person governs him- or herself in a way that shows a lack of concern with the justifiability of his or her actions, or an indifference to considerations that justi-fiable standards of conduct require one to attend to. What is more difficult is to describe the kind of response on the part of others that this impairment makes appropriate.

In the case of friendship, if a person lacks the attitudes required to be a friend, then in the extreme case this makes it appropriate not to regard him or her as a friend—to abandon, or not to form, the intentions and attitudes that friendship in-volves. In less extreme cases, a friend's deficiencies make it appropriate to qualify these intentions and attitudes, or perhaps to withhold *some* of them.

One view, which might be called moral retributivism, holds that an analogue of this more extreme reaction is appropriate in the case of the moral relationship: when people's moral deficiencies are great, the proper response on our part is to see even their most basic moral claims on the rest of us as limited and qualified. This view will hold that even our intentions not to kill or harm others are appropriately suspended toward those who fail to manifest these intentions toward others.[15]

I believe that this view is substantively mistaken. We would, ideally, like our moral relationship with others to be mutual. This relationship is fully realized when we are moved to act in a way that is justifiable to others and this concern is also reciprocated. But, in contrast with the case of friendship, the basic forms of moral concern are not conditional on this kind of reciprocation. Even those who have no regard for the justifiability of their actions toward others retain their basic moral rights—they still have claims on us not to be hurt or killed, to be helped when they are in dire need, and to have us honor promises we have made to them. Special circumstances, such as self-defense, may sometimes justify abrogating these rights, but moral deficiencies do not justify their general suspension.[16]

This poses a problem for the view of blame that I am advocating. If neither the basic concern with justifiability to a person nor the intention to respect that person's most basic substantive moral claims is modified by a person's deficiencies as a participant in moral relations, what room is there for blame as I am describing it—that is to say, for any modification, on our part, of the intentions, dispositions, and expectations that constitute our moral relationship with such a person? One possibility is to find room for this modification in the realm of moral emotions or similar attitudes. According to a view of this kind, what moral deficiencies make appropriate is just moral disapproval (a kind of grading) or more specific moral emotions such as resentment (and, in the case of one's own deficiencies, guilt).

I do not deny that these attitudinal responses can be appropriate, and that they are elements of blame. But an account of blame that focused only on these elements would be too thin. Blame also involves other modifications of our attitudes toward a person, including changes in our readiness to interact with him or her in specific ways. There is a range of interactions with others that are morally important but not owed unconditionally to everyone. If a person has no regard for the justifiability of his or her actions to others (or, despite professing such a concern, constantly sees things in a way that gives weight only to his or her own interests), then it is quite appropriate to refuse to make agreements with that person or to enter into other specific relations that involve trust and reliance. In addition, friendship and the other specific relationships I have been discussing presuppose adequate moral relations. So deficiencies that impair moral relations also impair, or rule out, these specific relationships. Blame therefore involves a suspension, in varying degrees and in varying ways, of one's readiness to enter into these more specific relations, and suspension also of the friendly attitudes that signal a readiness to do so.

There is also room for modification in our intention to help others in certain ways. Some duties to aid are unconditional. Even murderers and rapists have a claim on us to be rescued when they are drowning or are in danger of bleeding to death after an accident. But normal moral relations also involve a general intention to help others with their projects when this can be done at little cost, and we need not have this intention toward those who have shown a complete lack of concern for the interests of others. It would be wrong of us to go out of our way to kick over their sandcastles, so to speak, but we need not offer them our shovels.

The attitudes on a person's own part that impair his or her relations with others also change the meaning of friendly greetings or expressions of helpfulness. Rather than expressions of moral identification, connectedness, or solidarity, they become one-sided actions, cases of turning a blind eye to something that ought not to be ignored. Such expressions may even be demeaning to the person who holds them, in the way that it is demeaning for a person to continue to treat someone as a loyal friend after learning that the "friend" has betrayed him or her.

Impairment of a person's moral relation with others can also make it appropriate to suspend the dispositions to feelings that I mentioned above as part of the normal moral relationship. The fact that a person has behaved very badly toward you or toward others can make it appropriate not to take pleasure in that person's successes, and not to hope that things go well for him. Not being disposed to such hopes and feelings in regard to a person is not, however, the same thing as judging it to be good that things go badly for him or her (or even judging it not to be good that they go well). Hoping for something, or taking pleasure in it, is not the same thing as judging it to be good, as we saw earlier in the case of friendship: hoping that one's friend will win the prize and being disposed to take special pleasure in her success need not involve judging it to be better that she should win. The failure to draw this distinction, between what one has reason to hope for and what would be objectively better to have happen, can lead one to the mistake of taking the appropriateness of suspending the disposition to hope things go well for a person as evidence for a desert-based retributivism, according to which it is good that those who do wrong should suffer.[17]

One should also bear in mind here the distinction I have drawn between blameworthiness and blame. To claim that a person is blameworthy for an action, I have said, is to claim that his action indicates something about that agent's attitudes toward others that impairs his relations with them. To blame someone is to hold attitudes toward him that differ, in ways that reflect this impairment, from the attitudes required by the relationship one would otherwise have with the person.

A judgment of blameworthiness is one that anyone can make, however distant he or she may be from the relevant agent and action. But the content of *blame* depends on the significance, for the person doing the blaming, of the agent and of what he has done.[18] Blame has the most substantial content for people who interact with the agent in some way, as friends or family members, or as neighbors or coworkers or fellow citizens. This is so, first, because they are most likely to be affected by the impairment in question and the action that expressed it, and, second, because they need to decide what intentions to have regarding their future interactions with the agent, and what meaning to assign to those interactions.

The appropriate response will thus depend on the person's exact relation to the blameworthy action and the attitudes it reveals. Different responses will be appropriate, for example, if one is oneself the victim or intended victim of the action, or one is someone whom the agent apparently would see as an appropriate object of similar treatment (someone of the same gender or race as the victim, for example).[19]

Because the content of blame depends in this way on the significance of the agent and the agents' faults for the person doing the blaming, its content is attenuated in the case of agents who lived long ago and have no significance for or effect on our lives. We can judge such people to be blameworthy, but such a judgment has mainly vicarious significance, as a judgment about how it would have been appropriate for those closer to the agent to understand their relations with him.[20] It may imply, for example, that those who interacted with this person had good reason to withdraw their intentions to trust or rely upon him. But the idea that we ourselves *blame* him for what he did can sound somewhat odd. As our distance from a person increases, blame becomes simply a negative evaluation, or attitude of disapproval, and even this evaluative element can seem pointless grading unless we have some particular reason to be concerned with what the person in question was like.

Disapproval may be all that blame can amount to for someone taking an entirely detached and impartial point of view.[21] But we need not always have a detached attitude toward agents who are distant from us in space and time. We can be injured by the wrongful action of someone we have never met and never will meet; perhaps someone who lived long before we were born. In such a case it makes sense to say that we blame that person for bringing about the injury. This might be explained by saying that there is a special relationship, in the relevant sense, between perpetrators and their victims. In a way this is right, but it cannot be the whole story, since *that* relationship itself cannot be the one that is "impaired" by what the perpetrator does. Rather, the victim's relation to the perpetrator is impaired relative to the standard relationship between persons generally, insofar as the perpetrator's action showed a failure to have the concern for the welfare of others that is part of what we all owe to each other.

Being the victim of an action by some stranger makes it the case that that person has had a distinctive role in our life, as the author of an event that we have to come to terms with. It thus gives our attitude toward that person a distinctive significance, even if we will never interact with that person in the future and therefore do not need to decide how to behave toward him or her. The fact that some historical agent, such as Hitler, caused terrible harm for people we know, or their families, can also give blame greater significance. As I will argue below in the section on the ethics of blame, it can be blameworthy—that is to say, impair our relations with others—not to blame agents who harmed them. In such cases even the evaluative element in blame is far from pointless.

The distinction between the moral seriousness of the impairment indicated by what an agent does and the significance of this impairment for a person who stands in a certain relation to the agent also provides the basis for an explanation of the phenomenon of moral outcome luck. Consider first a case of what I called above objective stigma.

> Person A always drives carefully. Nonetheless, one evening as A is driving home, a child runs in front of his car and is killed.

The fact that A is the one who killed the child has an effect on what it is like for others, especially the child's parents, to interact with him in normal ways. It changes what it is like for the parents to stand next to A at the bus stop, to say hello to him in the morning, or to rely on him, as a member of the neighborhood babysitting pool, to take care of their surviving children. This is so even if they fully believe that A was not at fault, and blame is therefore not appropriate. My account shows how objective stigma is *similar* to blame even though it is not the same thing: both involve a modification of one's relations with a person, a change in the meaning of one's interactions. Consider now genuine cases of moral luck.

> Person B is disposed to be reckless (not to be sufficiently concerned about the risks that his conduct poses to others), but he never actually endangers anyone because he never has the occasion to engage in risky conduct.

> Person C has the same disposition as B, but she drives a car. She drives recklessly but, through sheer good luck, injures no one.

Person D has the same characteristics as B and C, drives in exactly the same manner as C, but is unlucky and kills a child.

B's relations with others are impaired by his lack of regard for their safety. He is open to criticism on this account. But (assuming that his recklessness does not affect other aspects of his relations with others) the fact that he would drive recklessly if he drove gives people little reason to revise their attitudes toward him. It affects his relations with them very little if at all.

C, by contrast, actually endangers people. So her defects of character have a significance for them that B's do not. It therefore makes sense for them to revise their attitudes toward C: not only to stay out of her way and not loan her their cars, but also to regard her not as a "fun person" whose foibles should be shrugged off, but as person whose priorities are a threat to them and need revision.

D's faults have greater significance than C's for those who are affected by his driving: he is not only the person who killed a child but also the person whose recklessness led to the child's death. The fact that his fault has played this significant role in their lives raises a greater question about how they are going to understand their relations with him.

Given that the difference between D's case and C's is due to factors beyond their control, one might ask how the blame that is appropriate in the two cases can be different. If blame were *just* an evaluative attitude toward an agent's character, then we would, as Nagel says, have no reason to blame them differently.[22] After all, there is no difference in their character, or in the way it is expressed in what they do. Based on the view of blame I am proposing, however, one can have reason to treat the cases differently.[23] As I interpret it, blame is not a mere evaluation but a revised understanding of our relations with a person, given what he or she has done. Blame is therefore a function not only of the gravity of a person's faults but also of their significance for the agent's relations with the person who is doing the blaming. The outcome of D's action may be due in part to bad luck, but it is also due to a *fault* on D's part. It therefore increases the significance of that fault for those who have been affected by it. What is involved in D's case is thus not just the phenomenon involved in C's case plus that involved in A's. Rather, the causal outcome of D's action multiplies the significance of his fault. In A's case, by contrast, there is nothing of moral significance to multiply.[24]

The differences, and similarities, in the appropriate reactions to A and to D can be brought out by considering the role that apology, or something like it, can have in these cases. Saying "I'm sorry" is appropriate even in A's case. But in his case this would not be an apology but an expression of regret at the tragic outcome of his action. Its function would not be to admit a fault but rather to reaffirm that there was no fault—no lack of concern on A's part for the safety of others—and to invite the parents of the child to acknowledge this, thereby helping to ease the difficulty in their relationship caused by the unlucky outcome. In D's case, on the other hand, a genuine apology is called for. Its function would be to acknowledge his fault, to acknowledge the significance of this fault for those affected by it, and to express the wish to repair his relationship with them.[25]

It is common to speak of blame as a form of "moral appraisal" or "moral evaluation," and to speak of praise and blame as if they were positive and negative versions of the same thing: similar attitudes with opposite valences. But as I am suggesting we should understand blame, it is not just a negative evaluation or appraisal of a person but a particular understanding of our relations with him or her.[26] And if praise is the expression of a positive appraisal, it is not the opposite of blame as I interpret it. This raises the question of what the positive correlate of blame would be.

The clearest example is gratitude. Gratitude is not just a positive emotion but also an awareness that one's relationship with a person has been altered by some action or attitude on that person's part. Sincerely felt, this entails having the reciprocal attitudes that this changed relationship makes appropriate. Typically, this involves a readiness to respond in kind—for example, a greater readiness to help a person who has gone out of her way to help you, should the occasion arise.

The things that one can properly be grateful for are not limited to actions. One can be grateful for a person's concern when one is ill or going through some difficult and stressful event. One's relationship with a person can be changed by the fact that she felt this special concern, even if her expression of it did not help one in any way.

It can be appropriate to be grateful to a person, and more disposed to help her, simply because she tried very hard to help you, even if her efforts did not succeed. This raises the question (parallel to the question of blame and moral outcome luck, discussed above) of whether it is appropriate to be more grateful to a person who succeeded in helping you than to someone else who tried just as hard to do so but failed, through no fault of her own. If gratitude were, like praise, a form of evaluation, then it would seem that there can be no difference in the appropriate responses in these cases. However, my relationship-based view allows room for a difference, since being benefited as a result of someone's exceptionally generous attitudes (like being harmed by his recklessness) changes one's relationship with him or her. But in what way should this make a difference in one's response? My own sense is that it does not make a difference in the degree to which one should have an increased readiness to help him or her in return. The question is whether something more is called for in the case of successful help—a gift, perhaps, or some other acknowledgment of the benefit one has received.

Some Strengths and Weaknesses of My Account

The account that I have been presenting explains several aspects of the relation between wrongness and blame. It explains why not every instance of wrongness is blameworthy and not every blameworthy action need be impermissible. It also explains why the blameworthiness of an action depends on the reasons for which a person acted, in ways that, as I have argued in earlier chapters, impermissibility does not. The agent's reasons for acting (and the fact that other considerations did not count for him as reasons against so acting) are what constitute his attitude toward others, and what have the implications that blame involves, in the account I am offering.

It follows from the way in which blame depends on an agent's reasons that conditions under which an agent acted, such as extreme stress or fear, can affect blame insofar as they affect the degree to which the action reflects the agent's actual attitudes. It also follows that blame does not come merely in degrees of more or less but varies in countless ways, corresponding to the different ways in which our understanding of a person and his attitudes toward others can vary. As I have already pointed out, the content of blame—the implications that an agent's conduct has for one's relations with him or her—can also vary from person to person, depending on one's relation to the agent and action in question.

The question of what our relations with a person are or should be—what attitudes we should have toward her—directs our attention to facts about her that are naturally called aspects of her character. So the account I am offering explains why blame should be seen as involving assessment of a person's character. But by placing this assessment within the context of our relations with a person, my account explains why this assessment is not pointless grading, or purely prudential calculation. It also explains why only some aspects of character are relevant grounds for blame. Lack of ambition may be a fault of character, but in the account I am proposing it is not *in itself* grounds for blame by others. We might blame a person for his lack of ambition because this led him to let his family down, but this would actually be blame for violating his family obligation. Blame for the character flaw itself makes sense only for someone who stands in some relation to the person for which this characteristic is important: a coach or teacher, for example, might blame a student for lack of ambition. Blame in such a case would naturally consist in some modification of the attitudes that the relationship involves, such as a decreased willingness to help the student perfect his or her skills.

One can also blame *oneself* for one's own lack of ambition, or for other faults or transgressions. The very idea of blaming oneself may seem at first to present a difficulty for my account of blame, which emphasizes the defective character of the blamed person's relations with *others*. But this is not in fact a problem. To begin with, my account can easily allow for the fact that one can take oneself to be *blameworthy* for lacking proper concern for others. One can make a judgment of blameworthiness about oneself as well as about anyone else, friend or stranger. In all these cases this is a judgment about how the blamed person's relations with others are impaired. But when the person is oneself, and the judgment is about one's own relations with others, specifically about the attitudes they have reason to hold toward one, this gives rise to special concern, regret, and a desire to change things. These responses constitute *blame* of oneself: because of one's own attitudes toward and treatment of others, one can no longer endorse one's own feelings and actions, but must instead endorse the criticisms and accusations made against oneself by others. One cannot, so to speak, be one's own friend.

This kind of estrangement is uncomfortable, and it is therefore tempting to avoid it by continuing to endorse one's attitudes—to love oneself wholeheartedly—despite the recognition that one is blameworthy. "What a rascal I am!" such a person might say, with an indulgent smile. This kind of divergence between a judgment of blameworthiness and the adjustment of attitude that it calls for is the first-person analogue of a person who continues to be friends with someone who treated her badly. But in this case the divergence—the failure to take one's own faults seriously—can impair one's relations with those one has wronged, and thus itself be blameworthy.

One can also blame oneself for faults, such as lack of ambition, even when they do not affect others. This is like the moral self-blame I have just been discussing, in involving a kind of self-estrangement. But it differs because it arises simply from an impairment of the ground relationship with oneself—an inability to "count on" oneself—rather than from an impairment of relations with others.

There are also other forms of blame, dependent on particular ground relationships, that are continuous with moral blame but go beyond it. A shared commitment to a value or a cause, for example, can establish a special connection with someone whom one has never met, perhaps because this person lived long ago. Such a person may have a special place in our understanding of our own lives, as the person who developed a certain idea or who advanced in some way a goal to which we are committed. If we learn that in fact this person failed to live up to this value, or failed to fulfill the obligations of a member of this group, our relation with him or her will be impaired, the impairment being measured in comparison with the relation that we would hope or expect to have with someone with whom we share this value, history, or commitment. We will feel that this person was not a solid member of the group but was instead a slacker, a renegade, disloyal, or even a traitor—these all being species of blame relevant to these special relations.

The dependence of blame on relationships also explains what is special about blame of young children. We do not blame young children for things such as rudeness or self-centeredness in the same way that we would blame an adult. This is not because the relevant standards of conduct are different for children. We would not say to a child, "It is all right to hit people now, since you are a child, but don't do it later when you are grown up." The difference lies in the dimension of blame, not the permissibility. In some cases this difference can be explained by the fact that young children cannot be expected to understand the consequences of what they do—to foresee what these consequences will be or to understand their significance. For example, a child may not be able to understand why a certain remark is particularly rude or hurtful. So the willingness to make such remarks does not indicate the same deficiency in a child as it would in an adult. But this cannot be the full explanation. Even when children understand full well why they should not do something, they may not be blamed for doing it in the same way that an adult would be.

I believe that the explanation lies in the ways in which our normal relationship with a child (our own child or even someone else's) differs from our relationship with normal adults.[27] Our relationship with children is an unequal one because of the child's relative lack of development, including moral development. It is a tutelary relationship: we are to understand that children are "just learning" and to help them grow. Our relationships with children thus lack certain elements of our relationships with normal adults—we do not expect to be able to rely on children in certain ways, for example, and if they fail to be reliable, our relationship with them is not impaired. We may engage in expressions of blame toward them—or at least use words that normally express blame—but these words have a more purely educative function and do not indicate the same thing that they would in the case of an adult. If a young child hits people, for example, or can't keep a secret, this does not raise the question of whether we should write him off as someone we will not associate with. Knowing that we can't rely on a person not to do these things would constitute impairment of our relationship with an adult but not, at least not in the same way, with a child.

Some may object to the account of blame I am offering because it seems to them to be too weak or mild. Blaming someone, they would say, involves something more than taking one's relationship with that person to be "impaired" in the way I have described. If one has this reaction when considering blame from the point of view of the person doing the blaming, I suggest considering matters from the point of view of someone who is blamed. The realization that you have done something that gives others good reason to revise their understanding of their relationship with you, and that they also take this view, is a serious matter.[28] Moreover, this analysis seems to fit well with the experience of guilt: feeling guilty for something one has done is plausibly understood as feeling that it has impaired one's relationship with certain people. In my experience there is nothing weak or mild about such feelings.

Another natural objection to my view is that it does not account sufficiently for the fact that blame is always *for* some action.[29] On the interpretation I offer, a conclusion that someone is blameworthy is a conclusion about the significance of that person's attitudes for his or her relations with others. The person's willingness to perform a certain action can reveal these attitudes and thus provide evidence for such a conclusion. But we can reach conclusions about people's attitudes on other grounds, such as what they say, or approve of. So blame, as I am describing it, can be independent of any particular blameworthy action. (A purely evaluative account of blame, such as Hume's, has this same implication.)

There may be some tension here between my view and some of the things we are inclined to say about blame. But our ordinary ideas about blame are not entirely consistent on this point. It makes sense, for example, to say that we blame a person for being hard-hearted toward others, even if we base our assessment on his frequent remarks rather than on anything he has done. In such a case it is not just the remarks that we blame him for but also the attitudes they express, which would be blameworthy whether or not they were expressed (as is evident in our feelings about our own unexpressed attitudes).

Moreover, even in my own view there are several ways in which a person's actions have a special status as grounds for blame. As Adam Smith writes, "We are capable, it may be said, of resolving, and even taking measures to execute, many things which, when it comes to the point, we feel ourselves altogether incapable of executing."[30] Huckleberry Finn, for example, might well have maintained quite firmly that he would never help a runaway slave to escape, since that would be stealing. But when the occasion presented itself, he found that he could not turn Jim in. A willingness—or unwillingness—to act can show something about a person that we could not be certain of on other grounds.

Actions also have a special role in making blame (as opposed to judgments of blameworthiness) appropriate. The significance of blame, as I have said, depends on one's relation to the person being blamed. The fact that an agent has wronged a person gives that person and her friends and associates reasons to blame that agent that they do not have to blame other agents in the history of the world who are equally blameworthy. As I pointed out in discussing moral outcome luck, the fact that he has caused this harm gives that agent a special role in their lives. It raises the question of what attitude they are to have toward him and thus gives a point to their blaming him, a point that would not exist in relation to people with whom they have had no interaction.

The attitudes of a person with whom one has to interact on a regular basis can also raise this question, however, in a way that need not depend on a particular blameworthy action. We have to decide how to understand our relations with such a person, and what meaning to attach to our interactions. There can thus be a point to revising these understandings—to blaming the person—because of his or her attitudes, even if this is not blame for a particular action.

Blame is concerned with something that has already happened. It attributes a certain kind of significance to what a person has done. What has been done can't be changed, but it is interesting to ask what, if anything, a person who is the subject of blame could do to modify, or even erase, the significance of what has happened. I have just mentioned the possibility of reinterpretation, of arguing that the action does not have the significance claimed for it. But if no reinterpretation is plausible, what can be done to change things? This brings us to the question of forgiveness, and how it is possible. If my account of blame is correct, forgiveness involves the restoration of an impaired relationship, perhaps in modified form. What forgiveness requires is some change in attitude on the part of the blamed person that makes this restored relationship one that all parties can endorse.[31]

It is a strength of my account of blame that it fits naturally with a plausible view of forgiveness. But this account of forgiveness shares a feature of my interpretation of blame that might seem to be an objection to both accounts, namely that that they do not give a central role to moral emotions such as resentment. It may be thought that forgiveness is mainly a matter of putting an end to resentment and other hostile feelings—without these, there is nothing for forgiveness to do—and that, correspondingly, blame essentially involves having feelings of this kind. Both of these claims seem to me mistaken. If I "write someone off" as a person I am going to have nothing to do with, then I am blaming him, even if this is accompanied by no hostile feelings, perhaps because I regard him as not worth being angry at.[32] And when someone has been "written off" in this way, even without anger or resentment, there is certainly something for forgiveness to do.

Is Blame Limited to Individual Human Agents?

The view of blame I am proposing can explain how and when it can make sense to blame agents other than individual human beings, such as countries, institutions, firms, or groups. Consider first, for purposes of contrast, the possibility of blaming inanimate objects. Suppose my basement flooded because the sump pump failed. If it turns out that this happened because a piece of debris became lodged in the pump, you might say that I should not blame the pump. This might be interpreted, in my view, as a claim that I should not take this failure as a reason for revising my attitude toward the pump, and the relevant attitude would be one of trust or reliance. If the pump had simply stopped working, then I would have had reason to revise this attitude, but in the present case, the suggestion is, I do not.

We do sometimes have sentimental feelings toward pieces of equipment that have provided us with long and "faithful" service, such as an old car that always starts in the morning, no matter how cold it gets. This is sentimentality because the only form of "trust" that applies in these cases, as in that of the pump, is mere expectation. Genuine trust is not mere expectation but expectation grounded in a supposed responsiveness to certain reasons, or at least feelings, such as loyalty, sense of duty, or concern for others' welfare. Cars can be reliable but not faithful, because they do not have feelings or respond to reasons. So with respect to inanimate objects, we can speak of faithfulness, trust, and, I would say, blame only in a metaphorical sense.

Blame of collective agents such as countries, corporations, and other institutions might be understood in a similar thin sense. But blame of entities of this kind is often taken to have more moral content than this. My account of blame entails that, in order for such blame to have moral content, we need to attribute attitudes to these entities—attitudes such as feelings toward others or responsiveness to reasons—to which our attitudes toward them are in turn responsive.

It makes no sense to attribute feelings or emotions to countries or other collective agents, unless what is meant is just that most of the individual members have these feelings. Somewhat surprisingly, it makes more sense to see such entities, under appropriate conditions, as being responsive to reasons. This makes sense if two conditions are fulfilled. First, the entity must be a collective agent—that is, there must be procedural or other criteria for what constitutes a decision or action on its part. Second, those decisions or actions must exhibit the right kind of regularities: when considerations that provide a certain reason for action are present, the entity must generally act in a way that the reason makes appropriate. For this to be true nonaccidentally, the entity must be organized in a way that we can see it as receiving information of the relevant kind, and processing it in a way that regularly affects its decisions.

This account is entirely neutral as to the content of the reasons in question. They might be reasons having entirely to do with narrow goals that might be taken to define institutional self-interest. But responsiveness of this sort to reasons of the right kind, such as the safety or well-being of a certain group of people, could provide the basis for an attitude of trust toward a collective agent that would go beyond mere expectation. Actions that showed the entity to be indifferent to these reasons could then impair this trust and thus be the basis for blame, as I am interpreting it.

An example may help to illustrate this idea of blame of collective agents and its relation to blame of individual human agents.[33] Suppose that a ferry sinks and many people die. Two questions might be raised: Do we have grounds to blame the ferry company? Do we have grounds to blame any of the individuals involved? I believe that in this case these two questions correspond roughly to: Do we have grounds to suspend our trust of the ferry company (say, by revoking its license to operate ferries) because it is insufficiently responsive to relevant considerations (of safety)? And do we have grounds to suspend our trust in any of the individuals involved (for example by firing them or suspending their licenses to serve in the positions they occupy)?

These questions are parallel in structure but independent of each other to a significant degree. They might both merit the same answer, but need not do so. If the accident was due to an irresponsible decision made by one person (the head of maintenance, who allowed the ferry to sail when it was disabled, or the captain, who should not have left port given the bad weather), then this person should be blamed (perhaps fired or suspended from his job). The answer to the other question then depends on whether the company's hiring and supervisory procedures should have screened out this person as unreliable, or whether it should have had fail-safe procedures in place that would have prevented a bad decision by one person from going into effect.

It is also possible that no individual was at fault. For example, perhaps the maintenance people who knew that the ferry was disabled did pass on this information in the proper way, but owing to bad internal communications within the company, the information never reached the people in charge of scheduling departures or the crew operating the ferry itself. If this was so, then it might show that the company is organized in a way that makes it untrustworthy—insufficiently sensitive to relevant information to be relied upon to operate ferries safely. But none of the individuals I have mentioned would be to blame. (It is a further question whether someone higher up in the company is properly to blame because he or she should have detected the flaws in the way information is handled within the company.)

Some wariness about the idea of relationships of trust and loyalty toward large organizations is certainly in order. Corporations spend millions trying to get us to have such attitudes toward them, and it may seem worse than sentimental to think of oneself as having a "relationship" with the manufacturer of one's dishwashing liquid. But it is not implausible to say that we trust some companies not to put substances that there is reason to believe are harmful into their products, and that if we learned that some company knowingly did this, then we would no longer think of it as a respectable participant in the market. This kind of blame presupposes trust as the alternative, default relationship against a given relationship is measured.

We should distinguish here between two kinds of skepticism about collective blame. The first is skepticism about whether it ever makes sense to attribute attitudes to collective agents and to have reciprocal attitudes toward them ourselves. The second is skepticism about whether certain attitudes in particular—such as trust—are warranted toward particular collective agents, or toward collective agents of particular kinds, such as business corporations. Skepticism of the latter sort is certainly in order in many cases. But only skepticism of the former kind is at odds with the possibility of blame of collective agents, understood in the way I have proposed.

The possibility of blaming collective agents seems clearest when one moves away from entities such as soap companies to collective agents that purport to be guided by noncommercial aims, and when one considers blame by individuals whose relation to these agents is something closer than that of consumer with producer. One might, for example, be pleased to work for a university or nonprofit organization because of its supposed commitment to certain values. But if it turned out that this institution was not responsive to the values it claimed to be serving, or even acted contrary to those values, then one would no longer have the same reason to "identify with it," to be willing to sacrifice for it, or to take pride in contributing to it. This would be a clear case of blame as I am proposing we should understand it.

A collective agent can be responsive to reasons in the sense that I have described, and hence be a possible object of blame in the sense I am proposing, only if there are procedures through which it can make institutional decisions. Mere collections of people that do not meet this condition, such as ethnic groups, cannot be objects of blame on the account I am proposing. Since they do not make collective decisions that indicate responsiveness to reasons, there is no basis for attributing attitudes to such groups in anything other than the distributive sense, in which saying that the group holds certain attitudes is simply to say that most of its members do. This is just stereotyping.

Another issue to be considered under this heading is the possibility of blame in regard to nonhuman animals. Here there are two questions: the possibility of blaming nonhuman animals and the possibility of blaming humans for their treatment of animals. With regard to the first question, blame is possible if there is a relationship that can be impaired by the animals' conduct. A large part of the point of having pets lies in the relations of mutual trust and affection that we have, or imagine that we have, with them. This relationship also provides the basis for blame: if you decide that you can no longer trust your dog, or that your dog does not really care about you, this is a form of blame, in my view. But it is implausible to think that we have this kind of relationship with animals in general, including wild animals. So we cannot blame them for what they do to us.

The absence of such a relationship does not mean, however, that we cannot blame ourselves, or others, for our treatment of animals. Blame in these cases is a response to conduct or attitudes that impair our relationships with other humans, or with ourselves. If we believe that the suffering inflicted on animals in factory farming, for example, is something very bad, then our failure to respond to this disvalue can be the basis of guilt, as I am understanding it—it can impair our ability to identify wholeheartedly with our own attitudes and decisions.

The Ethics of Blame

One advantage of a relationship-based account of blame is that it can offer a good explanation of what might be called the ethics of blame—that is to say, of reasons why one can be open to moral criticism for blaming someone or for failing to blame them.

Consider, first, cases in which a person is open to moral criticism for blaming. It is obviously objectionable to blame someone unfairly, that is to say on insufficient grounds, and it seems true to say, more generally, that one should not be too quick to blame others but should instead show a "generosity of spirit" and be understanding and forgiving.[34] Some would go further, and say that blame is a moralistic and excessively "judgmental" attitude that it would be morally better to avoid altogether. Perhaps this is too saintly—more than most of us can manage—but it would be better to avoid blame if we could.

This view may draw some of its plausibility from the idea that blaming is a matter of judging others—giving them a low moral grade, so to speak. Understood in this way, blaming seems to involve adopting an unattractive position of superiority, as a moral judge of others. But blame does not have this character when it is understood in the way I am proposing. On the account I am offering, blame requires a moral judgment but it is not a matter of grading. It involves adopting attitudes toward a person that one takes to be called for by the significance that that person's action has for one's relationship with him or her. Since these relationships are in most cases symmetrical, blame involves no claim of superiority. Rather, it is made from within relationships that are generally between equals, and can even be required by these relationships.

Even when it is understood in this way, blame may still seem to have a disagreeable aspect. It may seem too much like nursing a grudge, and therefore to be something it would be better to avoid if one could. But this is a mistake. Blame can be carried to excess, but the complete rejection of blame would rule out important relations with others. Moreover, this rejection itself is likely to involve objectionable attitudes of superiority or inferiority.

To see why this is so, it will be helpful to start from the analysis of forgiveness put forward by Pamela Hieronymi. She takes up the problem of how it can be possible to forgive someone without denying (1) that what the person did was wrong, (2) that he or she is the kind of being who is responsible for her actions, and (3) that you have standing to complain about being treated in such a way.[35] Hieronymi argues that this problem can be solved, provided that the person who is to be forgiven acknowledges the wrongness of what she did and takes steps to reestablish her relations with the injured party on an acceptable footing.

The complete rejection of blame would amount to an expectation or requirement of unconditional forgiveness. In this case I can see no solution to the problem Hieronymi describes. Assuming that one's relationship with a person has requirements that he or she can fall short of, the rejection of blame would involve either denying that the other person's actions can have a meaning that impairs this relationship or denying that when this happens some adjustment in one's own attitudes is appropriate. The former (a denial of condition 2) involves an attitude of superiority toward the person in question (something like the attitude of a parent toward a very young child) and thus represents a failure to take that person seriously as a participant in the relationship. The latter (denial of condition 3) involves adopting an attitude of inferiority that is demeaning to oneself.

Cases of this latter kind are instances of a broader class in which failing to blame an agent for an action impairs one's relations with the victim of that action. Suppose that Powers has done something terrible to Vincent. If you know of this, and understand what a terrible thing it was, then your relationship with Vincent is impaired if you do not blame Powers—that is to say, if your intentions and expectations in regard to Powers remain those that you would have toward any respectable member of the moral community. It is not enough just to acknowledge that what Powers did was wrong. Given what Powers has done to Vincent, you cannot have unimpaired moral relationships with both of them at the same time. Failures to blame that involve denial of Hieronymi's condition 3 are special cases of this broader phenomenon—cases in which the person who is blaming or failing to blame is also the victim.

Not only blame but also some public expression of blame seems to be called for in cases of mass murder or gross violations of human rights. This is why victims of such crimes, and their families, object so strongly when the perpetrators are not punished and continue to be treated as ordinary members of society. Their claim is not just that it is appropriate to feel indignation and resentment toward such people, or that it is appropriate that they should be made to suffer (although many victims may also want this). The point is also that there is something inappropriate about being asked to treat them as respectable fellow citizens, and to accept others' treating them in this way.

It might be said that failure to blame is open to moral criticism in some cases because one owes it to agents to blame them, and in other cases because one owes this to their victims. But this is not quite right. What one "owes" these agents is not to blame them but only not to withhold blame on certain grounds. More exactly, it can be blameworthy (because it involves an impaired relation with a person) to excuse him or her from blame on the ground that he or she is not a responsible agent whose actions have meaning.[36] And it can be blameworthy (can involve an impaired relation with a person) to fail to blame agents who wrong that person on the ground that he or she is not the kind of being that is entitled to complain of such treatment.[37]

Whether or not failing to blame in either of these two ways is impermissible, both can be blameworthy. The attitudes that are taken to exclude blame in these cases are incompatible with important relations with others, or with oneself. When these attitudes are justified—when the person who might be blamed is in fact incapable of meaningful action, or when the person who might blame has no standing to complain—we do not have the relationships with the person that these attitudes would impair. But when these attitudes are unjustified, it is reasonable to object to them as impairing important relations (with oneself or others), which means that one is blameworthy for having them. This is an instance of the more general fact that not only wrongful actions but also attitudes themselves can be blameworthy (that is, can indicate impaired relations). It also illustrates the fact that one can be blameworthy for things that are not possible objects of choice, to which the question of permissibility therefore does not apply.

I have been considering the ways in which proper relations with agents or victims can rule out wholesale exclusion of blame. But there are also cases in which our relations with agents count against blaming them, or require one to qualify or modify blame. One such case is that of parents and their adult children. Even when parents must admit that what their grown son or daughter has done is blameworthy, it may be appropriate for them, as parents, to continue to offer sympathy and the right kind of encouragement, to look for the best in their offspring, and to be willing to trust them by "offering a second chance." These attitudes can be required of good parents even if strangers could properly regard their son or daughter as someone not to be associated with.

There is of course such a thing as being *too* willing to overlook the faults of one's children, as well as being insufficiently willing to do so. One might say that the proper course is determined by balancing the demands of one's relationship with one's child, the perpetrator, against the demands of one's relationship with the victim. But this metaphor of balancing is inadequate for a number of reasons.

First, seeing oneself as a parent (and as having reason to be a good one) involves seeing oneself as having reason to do the things I have mentioned: reason to offer sympathy and encouragement to one's offspring even (perhaps especially) when they have gone wrong, reason to look for the best in them, and reason to try to trust them by giving a second chance rather than "writing them off" as one might a stranger. Second, insofar as one has good reason to think of oneself as (normatively, not just biologically) a person's parent, and as having reason to be a good one, one actually *has* the reasons just listed. Third, if what a person has done is sufficiently bad, it may undermine the antecedent of the previous statement: it may provide grounds for morally disowning him or her. But the relation of parenthood is quite robust and unconditional, less easily undermined than friendship and some other relations.

Fourth, the reasons I have mentioned limit what others can reasonably demand of a parent. Victims can reasonably ask parents to acknowledge the legitimacy of their claims, and the blameworthiness of what their offspring have done. But they cannot reasonably ask parents to distance themselves from their offspring in the way that a stranger could be expected to. So the incompatibility between normal relations with perpetrators and normal relations with their victims, which I mentioned above at the end of the discussion of Powers and Vincent, is modified when the person being asked to blame is a parent of the wrongdoer.

So, fifth, in determining what can be expected of a parent by way of blame, two questions need to be asked. We should ask whether the wrong is so serious as to undermine the normative relation of parenthood. And if it is not, we should ask what kind of loyalty and support a good parent is called on to provide. The answer to each of these questions depends, to some extent, on the blameworthiness of what the son or daughter has done, and therefore corresponds to the strength of the claims of the victim. But these are questions about the requirements and limits of the relationship of parenthood, rather than ones that are to be answered by balancing this relationship against some competing value.

The fact that one's relations with others may limit the

possibility of revising one's intentions in the way that I say blame involves may seem to be a problem for my view.[38] It may seem that there are cases in which blame is clearly appropriate but there is no room for the revision of attitudes that constitutes blame as I am interpreting it. Suppose, for example, that my twenty-two-year-old son, who lives at home, drives carelessly and repeatedly dents and scrapes my car. It is quite appropriate for me to blame him for this, but what can this blame consist in, on my account? The natural thing would be for me to decide not to trust him with the car. But he needs the car to get to his job, so as a supportive parent I cannot refuse to lend it. It may therefore seem that the only room for blame in this case is a matter of negative evaluation (judging him to be careless) and moral emotion (feelings of resentment). I do not deny the relevance of these elements of blame, but I do not think that they are the most important part of what blame involves even in such a case. A relationship, in the sense I am concerned with, is a matter not only of what one does, or intends to do, but also of the reasons for which one does these things. Even if I have to go on letting my son use the car, this does not mean that I trust him. Rather, I let him use the car because I am obligated to do so, even though I do not trust him. I do not have the relationship with him that one could expect to have with a son of his age, one of sharing the use of family resources with a sense of mutual concern and responsibility. Our relationship is thus impaired, quite apart from any feelings of anger or resentment that I may have.

A similar analysis can explain how blame can be qualified by other special relationships, such as friendship, commitment to a common cause, and other bonds of loyalty. The answers to the two questions listed in my fifth point above will of course vary in these cases, depending on the relationship in question. In particular, answers to the first question (about the possibility of undermining these relations altogether) are likely to be different than in the case of parenthood, since other relationships may be more readily undermined or canceled by what a person has done.

Cases arise frequently in politics in which willingness to blame can be inhibited by loyalty, and failures to blame can themselves be blameworthy. Political leaders and those who speak for political parties and other groups are often unwilling to condemn wrongful actions by their compatriots, or members of their own party or ethnic group. If they are quite ready to blame others outside their group for similar wrongs, this refusal to blame may be criticized as inconsistent or hypocritical. But it can also be objectionable in another way. Unlike the relation between parent and child, the relation between members of a political party does not provide good reason for qualifying blame. Members of a party may have reasons of group pride or political calculation for maintaining solidarity by refusing to blame or break with members of their group who have committed crimes. But these justifications, unlike claims of parental loyalty, are ones that the victims of these crimes have no reason to accept. Refusing to blame in these cases is therefore incompatible with normal moral relationships with these victims. That is to say, it is blameworthy, although it may be in some cases a shrewd but cynical political tactic.

The blameworthiness involved in these cases is not a form of collective guilt, although it might be confused with it. The point is not that those who refuse to condemn crimes committed by members of their group thereby share the guilt for those crimes. It is rather that their relations with the victims are impaired in a related, albeit lesser, way. (It is lesser because a willingness to do unjustifiable things is a more serious impairment of one's relations with the victims than an unwillingness to condemn members of one's group for doing those things.)

I turn now from the question of who must blame to the question of who has standing to do so. I have argued that a judgment of blameworthiness is an impersonal one. It is a judgment that anyone can make, whatever his or her relation to the agents in question, while blame, as I interpret it, is more personal. Because it involves taking the view that a person's attitudes (usually, the attitudes revealed in what that person has done) impair one's relations with him or her, the content of blame varies, depending on what those relations are. The fact that blame depends on relationships in this way explains how a person's standing to blame can be undermined.

This undermining is clearest in cases in which the person who would do the blaming has in the past treated the person who is to be blamed in ways that are as bad as what that person is being blamed for. To take a mild example, suppose we are friends and that I am often extremely late for our appointments, for no good reason, and have sometimes failed to show up at all without giving you any warning. Suppose that on some occasion you fail to appear for our appointment and I complain indignantly, saying that friends ought not to treat each other this way. What I am saying may be quite true, but I am not in a position to make this complaint. It is not just that I am being inconsistent, applying to you a standard that I do not apply to myself, or that I am being hypocritical in applying to you a standard that my own conduct shows that I do not in fact accept. These things may be true, but there is also a further problem. I cannot claim that the attitudes revealed in your willingness to stand me up constitute an impairment in our relations, because the mutual expectations and intentions that constitute those relations were already impaired by my own similar attitudes, revealed repeatedly in my past conduct.[39] Things would be changed slightly if, when blaming you, I at the same time said, quite sincerely, that I was wrong to have behaved this way in the past. This would eliminate the inconsistency in my current judgments, but by itself it would not restore my standing to blame you. If anything could do that, it would have to involve something beyond just blaming myself, such as, at a minimum, giving convincing evidence that I recognize my faults and will behave differently in the future.[40]

A person's standing to blame can also be undermined by what he himself has done to people other than the person being blamed. Suppose that you have injured others by lying to them and stealing from them. If I am also guilty of lying and stealing, this undermines my ability to blame you for your actions.[41] As before, we might explain this by saying that it would be inconsistent or hypocritical of me to blame you. But something more is involved. In blaming you I would be holding that your willingness to behave in this way makes you someone toward whom I cannot have the intentions and expectations that constitute normal moral relations, such as the intention to trust you and rely on you. But insofar as these normal expectations and intentions are *mutual*, my own conduct already reveals me to be a person who cannot be a participant in these relations. I cannot be trusted in exactly the same way that you cannot. So there is something false in my suggesting that it is *your* willingness to act in ways that indicate untrustworthiness that impairs our moral relationship.

G. A. Cohen identifies several other ways in which a person's standing to blame can be undermined.[42] He observes, for example, that if you have told me to do something, ordered me to do it, or knowingly facilitated my doing it, then although you can correctly say that what I have done is wrong and blameworthy, you cannot blame me for doing it.[43] This can be explained in the same way as the cases I have just discussed. Your involvement in what I have done indicates a willingness to countenance the kind of thing I did. Therefore you cannot say that what stands in the way of your having possible moral relations with me is just *my* willingness to countenance such actions. Since these relations are symmetrical, your own willingness is just as much of an impediment.

Cohen also discusses a slightly different class of cases in which one person does something unjustifiable partly because another person has wrongfully deprived him of legitimate means for pursuing important goals. Even if this does not justify what the first person does, it bars the second person from blaming him for it. Suppose, for example, that you keep interrupting my meetings in order to force me to consider some complaint or proposal that you want me to consider. I may object to this behavior, quite correctly, on the ground that it is incompatible with the appropriate relations between us. I might say we ought to deal with such matters in a civil way, through the presentation of reasons, rather than by attempts at intimidation. I might be quite correct in saying this even if it is also true that I wrongfully refused to consider your case earlier, when you presented it in a civil manner. But if I did refuse, then I cannot now blame you for your behavior even if it is blameworthy. This is because I cannot claim that it is simply *your* attitudes that impair our relations with each other.

Cohen suggests that this explains why some governmental officials may lack standing to condemn terrorists. Even if what the terrorists do is unjustifiable, despite the legitimacy of their political goals, it may nonetheless be true that governmental officials lack standing to condemn these actions if their governments have prevented the terrorists from pursuing their goals by legitimate means. (This would not mean that the terrorists were not blameworthy: they might be appropriately blamed by the families of their victims, for example.)

Similar considerations explain how the fact that a person was treated terribly as a child can modify the way in which we can blame him for things that he does later, even if they are also terrible. I do not think that blame is undermined by the fact that a person had no control over the factors that made him the kind of person that he is, or by the fact that, given the kind of person he is, he is incapable of understanding the reasons against acting the way he does.[44] But even if the fact that a person was horribly mistreated as a child does not make it inappropriate to blame him by absolving him of responsibility, this factor can interact with blame in an important way. The fact that a person was mistreated can change our relation with him, in a way akin to those that Cohen discusses.

Gary Watson makes a similar point about the killer Robert Harris. Harris was unbelievably heartless and brutal. But when we learn how terribly he was treated as a child, Watson says, "we are unable to command an overall view of his life that permits the reactive attitudes to be sustained without ambivalence . . . The sympathy toward the boy that he was is at odds with outrage toward the man he is . . . In fact, each of these responses is appropriate but taken together they do not enable us to respond overall in a coherent way."[45] As Watson says, the facts about Harris's past do not erase or diminish his blameworthiness. They do not change the fact that he is a heartless killer and someone whom we should never trust. But they add something to this description, complicating our response to him. It is not just that we feel sympathy for Harris (or for him when he was a child). It is rather that our revised relation with him is complicated by the fact that he was so ill-treated—not by us personally, but by "the moral community." This affects blame in something like the way that Cohen suggests. It does not undermine altogether our standing to blame, but it requires a more complex revision of our attitudes toward him. It raises a problem about the kind of blame that is called for.

Blame and Freedom

Many people believe that blame presupposes freedom, and thus that it is never appropriate to blame people if all of their actions are caused by factors outside of them, over which they have no control. What is not commonly explained is why this should be so—or rather, what it is about blame that entails this requirement of freedom.[46] In this section I will consider two possible explanations, which I call the *requirement of psychological accuracy* and the *requirement of adequate opportunity to avoid*. My aim is to examine these reasons for thinking that blame requires some kind of freedom and to see how they apply when blame is understood in the way I am suggesting. The requirement of psychological accuracy is straightforward. Insofar as blame depends on the reasons for which an agent acted, a judgment that blame is called for can be modified or undermined by factors that change our view of what those reasons were.[47] Mistaken belief and coercion are factors of this kind. The fact that a person acted in a way that caused harm to someone else may seem to indicate a blameworthy lack of concern for the other's interests. But the requirement of psychological accuracy bars us from drawing this conclusion if the agent reasonably believed (albeit mistakenly) that this action would not be harmful, or that it was necessary in order to prevent a much greater harm to the person.

Similarly, an agent who knowingly causes harm to another is blameworthy if he or she does this gratuitously, or out of indifference to that person's interest. But the agent may not be blameworthy, or may be subject only to a different and lesser form of blame, if she caused the harm only because someone threatened her with grave harm if she did not. So, for example, a bank teller faced with a credible threat of deadly force should not be blamed for giving cash to a bank robber.

It is sometimes said that coercion renders blame inappropriate in such cases because an agent acting under duress is not responsible for what she does. This seems to me a mistake. Coercion does not undermine responsibility; rather, what it does is to change what the agent is responsible for. A person who is coerced, such as the bank teller I mentioned, still acts, and acts for certain reasons. Such a person is thus *responsible* for what she does: that is to say, her action is fully attributable to her. The bank teller may even deserve commendation for handling a dangerous situation in a calm and careful manner.

Rather than undermining responsibility, what coercion may do is to modify the permissibility of an action or the kind of blame, if any, that it makes appropriate. In the case of the bank teller, for example, the threat of harm may justify her handing over the money, which would otherwise be wrong. And even when coercion does not render what a person does permissible, it may alter the kind of blame that is appropriate. It is one thing to inflict harm on another person gratuitously, another thing to do so (even unjustifiably) out of fear of harm to oneself. The first kind of change (in permissibility) occurs because coercion changes the reasons there are for doing what the agent did. Changes of the second kind (in blameworthiness) occur because coercion changes in the reasons on which the agent acted.

The requirement of psychological accuracy can thus explain how lack of freedom can render blame inappropriate, or modify the kind of blame that is called for. But this explanation applies only when, as in cases of coercion, the lack of freedom alters the relation between an action and the attitudes of the agent who performs it. As many have pointed out, the lack of freedom that would be entailed by a general causal determinism need not have this effect.[48] Even if our attitudes and actions are fully explained by genetic and environmental factors, it is still true that we have these attitudes and that our actions express them.

Compatibilists have sometimes concluded from this that it is simply a mistake to think that moral assessment requires freedom from determination by outside causes. Hume, for example, argued that the tendency to think that moral assessment is incompatible with causal necessity results from a failure to distinguish between what he calls the liberty of spontaneity and the liberty of indifference.[49] Hume believed that we lack the liberty of indifference: that our actions are governed by regular causal laws. Indeed, he said, moral appraisal depends on this, since it depends on there being regular connections between actions and the attitudes they express. But this does not mean that we lack the liberty of spontaneity—that we always act *unwillingly*. Laws of nature are not coercive.

Put in my terms, Hume seems to think that what he called "necessity" (causal determination of our actions) could undermine moral appraisal only by depriving us of the liberty of spontaneity, thereby conflicting with the requirement of psychological accuracy. He therefore thinks that since the existence of causal laws governing our actions does not have this effect, there is no conflict between moral responsibility and causal determination. This argument depends on the assumption that psychological accuracy is the only basis on which moral responsibility might require freedom. This may be so given Hume's account of blame, according to which it is just a sentiment of disapproval toward an agent's character. But if blame is understood in some other way, then psychological accuracy may not be the only reason for believing that blame requires freedom.

Galen Strawson, for example, believes that in order for it to be appropriate to blame a person for committing a vicious crime, it is not enough that that action should actually express reprehensible attitudes such as indifference toward the lives of others and a desire to make them suffer. The agent must also have consciously and explicitly chosen to be the kind of person who would have such attitudes and act from them.[50] Strawson believes this because of the particular kind of moral assessment that he has in mind: the kind of moral responsibility "such that, if we have it, then it *makes sense*, at least, to suppose that it could be just to punish some of us with (eternal) torment in hell and reward others with (eternal) bliss in heaven."[51]

It does seem to make no sense, or at least to be highly objectionable, for God to make people suffer an eternity of torment for their sins if God set things up in such a way that it was inevitable that they would have exactly those sins. The requirement of psychological accuracy would not be violated in such a case. The people who would be punished would really have the moral faults in question. So there must be some other reason why this punishment is so objectionable. What makes it objectionable, I suggest, is the fact that they could not in any way have avoided this terrible punishment.

It is important to understand the structure of the moral idea at work here, which I call the requirement of adequate opportunity to avoid. This requirement applies in cases in which someone has suffered a harm that people have, in general, a claim not to be subjected to. (I will call this claim "the underlying obligation.") If the person who has suffered such a harm protests that this obligation has been violated, it can be at least a partial response to this objection to say that he or she had ample opportunity to avoid the harm by choosing appropriately. More may be required to respond adequately to this protest, but at least in many cases this appeal to the opportunity to avoid is an important part of any adequate response.

In the case of hell, more surely is required. Setting things up so that some people will suffer an eternity of torment (when things need not be set up this way) requires substantial justification. It is not enough *just* to say that those who suffer could have avoided it by making reasonable choices. But giving people adequate opportunity to avoid this fate is at least a necessary condition. We need *at least* to be able to say to people who suffer this fate that they could have avoided it by choosing reasonably. So if the idea that the blameworthy are to be consigned to hell is to be defensible, people have to have adequate opportunity to avoid being blameworthy (at least in the way that entails hell as a punishment).

The requirement of adequate opportunity to avoid is not an idea of desert. The idea is not that it is fitting or appropriate that people who fail to choose wisely should suffer certain harms. It may be better that they not suffer them. The point is merely that if they do suffer these harms, then their complaint against those who allowed it to happen may be undermined if they had adequate opportunity to avoid this outcome by choosing appropriately, and that in at least some cases it is morally objectionable to allow these harms to occur unless those who suffer them had such an opportunity.

My subject here is not heaven and hell but the much milder idea of blame.[52] But even blame is something people have good reason to dislike. It may therefore be seen as something they have some claim not to suffer, and therefore as something to which the requirement of fair opportunity to avoid may seem to apply. This is particularly so if blame is seen as a sanction—a form of unpleasant treatment that requires justification and is justified by its effects on people's behavior.

This reasoning does not apply when blame is understood in the way I am proposing. To see why, consider first why it does not apply if blame is understood merely as a kind of negative evaluation or, as Hume suggests, a sentiment of disapproval. Even understood in this way, blame is something that people have reason to dislike. We don't want people to draw, or even to have good reason to draw, negative conclusions about our relations with them. And we have reason to want them not to draw such conclusions even if they are never expressed and never affect their behavior toward us in any way. But we have no claim against others that they not draw such conclusions, so long as they have good grounds for thinking them to be correct. Since we have no such claim, there is no need to appeal to the idea of our having had "adequate opportunity to avoid" being blamed. Psychological (and moral) accuracy provide all the justification that blame requires, when it is understood in this way.

The problem with this account of blame is that it does not do justice to the seriousness of blame for those who engage in it or for those who are its objects. Blame is more than an assignment of moral grades. Moreover, it might be suspected that the thinness of this evaluative interpretation of blame is what accounts for its failure to require "adequate opportunity to avoid," and that an interpretation that captured the seriousness that blame seems to have would trigger this requirement. The question, then, is how the "seriousness" or "weight" of blame should be understood.

One familiar way to give blame greater significance is to interpret it as a kind of sanction—a form of treatment that, because it is disliked, can be used to influence behavior.[53] But this suggestion suffers from two related problems. The first is that the idea that blame is a sanction does not in itself give blame greater weight or seriousness. It presupposes that blame is something that people have good reason to want to avoid, rather than providing, or adding to, an understanding of what this reason is. It might be said that something is added insofar as such accounts focus on *expressions* of blame, which are particularly unpleasant. No one likes being criticized. But if a purely evaluative interpretation fails to capture the significance of blame, it would also seem inadequate as an account of why people want to avoid being the objects of expressions of blame.

The second problem is that blame itself (apart from particular expressions of blame) seems to have a seriousness that goes beyond mere evaluation, and does not consist in its being a sanction or a judgment that a sanction is called for. Even most expressions of blame are not adequately understood as sanctions. Expressions of blame can influence behavior, but they generally have different aims, such as registering the fact that our relationship with a person has been changed by his conduct, initiating a process that may lead to restoration of this relationship, or just standing up for one's own dignity. These aims are in most instances our primary ones. Our aim in expressing moral blame is not, in general, to serve as enforcers of moral requirements.

The account I am offering explains how blame can have a seriousness that goes beyond mere evaluation and yet does not need the kind of justification that would involve a requirement of adequate opportunity to avoid. To blame a person is to have attitudes and intentions that are made appropriate by the way in which that person's faults impair one's relation with him or her. This can involve different things in different cases, including such things as withholding or modifying trust and reliance, seeing the person as not eligible, or less eligible, to be a friend or a participant in cooperative relations, changing the meaning one assigns to the person's actions and to one's inter-actions with him or her, or even ceasing to be disposed to be pleased when things go well for the person, and ceasing to hope that they will go well.

These elements of blame deprive a person of things that he or she has reason to want. But they are not things to which anyone has an unconditional claim. We do not owe it to any-one to trust him or be his friend no matter how he treats us, or to value or take seriously conversation with him no matter what reasons guide his decisions about what to say, or to take pleasure in his well-being no matter what his attitude may be toward others. These attitudes are appropriate only toward those whose attitudes make them appropriate. Where they are not appropriate, we need no further justification for withhold-ing them: there is no need to appeal to beneficial consequences of doing so, or to claim that the person had adequate opportu-nity to avoid this loss.

Things may be somewhat different with respect to some *expressions* of blame. The discomfort and distress that a par-ticular way of expressing blame would cause can be a reason against it that calls for some countervailing justification. And this justification may sometimes appeal in part to the fact (if it is a fact) that the person could have avoided being blamewor-thy in this way. It can be cruel to berate someone for faults that he could not help having, particularly if he is unable to see the force of the moral objections to what he has done.[54] But not all expressions of blame are open to such objections. It is not cruel to explain to a person why one cannot trust him any longer, even if he cannot help being untrustworthy.

My account of blame is a *desert-based* view, in the sense in which I believe that term should be understood. That is to say, I take blame to consist of attitudes toward a person that are justified simply by attitudes of that person that make them appropriate, and I hold that there is no need to appeal to other justifications such as the beneficial consequences of blaming or the fact that the person could have avoided being subject to blame.[55] Like refusals of friendship, blame is justified simply by what a person is like.

In earlier writing, I have taken a narrower and less favorable view of desert. In *What We Owe to Each Other,* I identified "the desert thesis" as "the idea that when a person has done something that is morally wrong it is morally better that he or she should suffer some loss in consequence," and I said that this view was "morally indefensible."[56] My present view of blame is not an instance of the desert thesis. The fact that someone has behaved wrongly can make it appropriate to withhold certain attitudes and relationships, and withholding these things may make that person's life worse. But withholding them is justified, in my view, by the fact that they have become inappropriate, not by the fact that withholding them makes the person worse off. Ceasing to hope that things go well for a person can be one element of blame, but as I have emphasized, this does not involve thinking it to be good that things not go well for him. Not even hoping that they go badly need involve this. (Just as hoping that one's friend will win the lottery need not entail thinking it would be better if one's friend won than if someone else did.)

I still reject the desert thesis. But it no longer seems to me helpful, or fair to the idea of desert, to identify desert with this particular thesis. There are other, much more plausible views that it makes sense to classify as desert-based because of their particular justificatory structure. My view in particular differs from moral retributivism not in its form (in the way it sees blame as justified in relation to underlying moral requirements) but rather in its content. Moral retributivism is implausible because it is implausible to hold that even the most basic moral requirements—such as the requirement not to inflict serious harm and to prevent such harm when one can—are conditional, and not owed to those whose attitudes impair their moral relations with others.

If blame involves only the alteration of attitudes that I have described, then it can be justified by appeal to the idea that this shift of attitudes is appropriate, or called for, by what an agent is like.[57] Justifications that appeal to the idea of what is "appropriate" or "fitting" are open to objection on the ground that they involve appeals to unstructured intuition, and unless supplemented in some way lack serious normative force. The view I am offering gives this idea more structure (thereby mitigating this objection, if not, to be sure, avoiding it altogether) by locating the idea of appropriateness within a conception of particular relationships, which explain the kind of normative force that is in question.[58] It is asking too much to demand that we be ready to enter into relations of trust and cooperation, and various forms of friendly relations, with people who have shown that they have no regard for our interests.

Doing so can even be demeaning. So an appeal to what is appropriate is an adequate explanation for the suspension of these attitudes. But it is much less plausible to appeal simply to what is "appropriate" to justify the infliction of suffering on those who have treated others badly, or even to justify refusing to help them when they are in danger. The idea of appropriateness by itself seems too weak to bear this justificatory weight.

The evident inadequacy of such a justification may be what draws defenders of moral retributivism toward incompatibilism. Because they see moral blameworthiness as entailing loss of one's claim to avoid suffering, they conclude that in order to be blameworthy it is not enough just to be a certain way; one must also have had adequate opportunity to avoid being that way. As Galen Strawson puts it, one must have consciously and freely chosen to be that way. This represents a move beyond what I am now calling a desert-based view to the idea of an adequate opportunity to avoid.

It is worth asking whether there is any other moral idea beyond the two I have mentioned (psychological accuracy and adequate opportunity to avoid) that might be thought to establish a moral link between blameworthiness and freedom. I do not believe that there is, but I will consider three ideas about what might pull one in this direction.

First, rather than being an appeal to the idea of adequate opportunity to avoid, the requirement that a person must have freely and consciously chosen to be the way he or she is might be internal to the relevant notion of desert: having so chosen might be part of what an agent must be *like* in order for blame to be appropriate. We should distinguish here between two interpretations of the idea of a person's having chosen to have certain characteristics.

The first interpretation employs the idea of choice in a purely psychological sense. A person chooses something in this sense if it comes about as a result of his having consciously opted for it on the basis of his actual preferences and values, perhaps as these seem to him on reflection. It might be said, however, that the fact that someone chose, in this sense, to have certain attitudes does not make those attitudes fully his, in the sense required for them to be the basis of moral assessment, if the attitudes on the basis of which this reflective assessment was made were not themselves chosen by the agent. This leads to the second interpretation, according to which the attitudes that are the basis of blame must, ultimately, be ones that are chosen by the agent in a deeper sense of "choice" that is independent of any factors that are not themselves ones the agent has chosen.[59]

As Galen Strawson argues, this deeper idea of choice is incoherent. A choice must be made on some basis that precedes that choice, and choice is significant because it reflects that basis, thereby expressing what the agent is like. Even if there could be a choice that lacked such a basis, it would lack significance because it would reflect nothing about the agent. There would be nothing to reflect.[60]

Strawson concludes from this that moral responsibility is impossible, whether we have free will or not. But the incoherence he identifies should also give us pause about the reasoning that led to the idea that the grounds of moral assessment must be chosen in this deeper sense. Why should we think that an agent's choice in the purely psychological sense is not a sufficient basis for moral assessment?

The answer may be that it is unfair to judge an agent on the basis of a choice that is itself based on attitudes that he or she has not chosen to have, because this leaves open the possibility that the agent is "trapped" by the psychological traits he or she happens to have.[61] If this is not an appeal to the lack of adequate opportunity to avoid blame (which I am setting aside for the moment), then it seems to be a deeper version of the requirement of psychological accuracy, which might be called a requirement of metaphysical accuracy. This requirement is based on the idea that there is a sense of "what a person is like" that is deeper than, and not settled by, the psychological attitudes that that person happens to have, and that blame and other forms of moral assessment must be based on what a person is like in this deeper sense.

If these assumptions are correct, then Hume was mistaken in thinking that the liberty of spontaneity that moral assessment involves did not also require the liberty of indifference. If we lack the liberty of indifference—if our psychological attitudes and the actions they lead to are governed by causal laws—then (on the assumptions we are considering) we also lack liberty of spontaneity of the kind that moral assessment requires, since there is no assurance that our psychological states will accurately reflect what we are like, at the deeper level with which moral assessment is concerned.

But should we accept these assumptions? I believe that we should not. I do not see how to understand the deeper sense of "what a person is like" that is supposed to be independent of the psychological attitudes that the person happens to have. Moreover, it is these attitudes that constitute our relations with each other and are therefore the basis of moral blame, as I am suggesting we understand it.

The question of whether a person's attitudes were chosen, or were subject to his or her control, might be seen as important for a further reason, however. The idea might be that an attitude is not attributable to a person—not his or hers in the sense required for it to be the basis of moral assessment—unless having that attitude is under the person's control, in the sense of being responsive to that person's considered judgment.[62] This is an appealing idea, but one that I believe is mistaken.[63]

For an attitude to be attributable to a person in the sense required for it to be an appropriate basis for blame or other forms of moral assessment, it is not necessary even that that attitude be under the person's control in the purely psychological sense of being responsive to his or her judgment. When something seems to me to be a reason, it is up to me to decide whether it is one. This is up to me in the sense of being a judgment that I am answerable for and can be asked to defend, but it is not, in general, up to me in the sense of being a matter of choice on my part. To have a choice whether to do A or B is to be in a position to make it the case that I do one or the other by deciding appropriately. Our decisions about reasons are not in general like this. We can choose whether to do A or B. But we *decide* (not choose) whether a given consideration is a good reason to do A, just as, in the realm of belief, we decide (not choose) whether a consideration is a reason to believe something.

Attitudes about reasons do not generally arise from conscious judgment, let alone from reflection. Most often, things simply strike us as reasons for certain actions, or as irrelevant to them, without our having given any prior thought to the matter. But although they arise unbidden and are not objects of choice, our attitudes toward reasons are, ideally, responsive to our judgment. If I were perfectly rational, then when I decided, on reflection, that a consideration that at first seemed to me to be a reason for a certain action was not in fact a reason, this consideration would cease to seem to me to be a reason. Our attitudes toward reasons are thus ideally, or normatively, under our control.

But what would hold ideally is not always true in practice. A consideration can continue to seem to me to be a reason even though I judge firmly that it is not one. The fact that hiring a certain candidate would please a colleague whom I dislike can continue to seem to me to be a reason to decide against that candidate, even though I firmly judge that it is not. It might be claimed that when an attitude resists a person's judgment in this way, and thus fails to be under his or her reflective control, it is not an appropriate basis for blame because it is not his or hers in the required sense.[64]

I do not believe that we generally take this view, however, or that we have good reason to do so. There is at least some reason for rejecting blame for the consequences of actions when these are beyond an agent's control: the fact that these consequences are beyond the agent's control may mean that they tell us nothing about his or her attitudes. But this reason clearly does not apply to the person's attitudes themselves. Even when they run contrary to the agent's judgment, they remain attitudes that he has.

Consider, for example, a man who firmly rejects racist views but who nonetheless sometimes finds himself thinking, when he sees people of a different race, that their skin color is a reason for regarding them as inferior and for preferring not to associate with them. We may suppose that when such a thought occurs to him he is appalled by it and he rejects these thoughts as mistaken and shameful. But they continue to occur nonetheless. The fact that these reactions are contrary to his considered judgment—that he "disowns them"—makes a significant difference to our assessment of this person. It changes the overall picture of what he is like. But it does not erase the relevance of these attitudes altogether. They are still attributable to him, and their occurrence is still a moral defect. That is why he is right to be disturbed and shamed by them. Perhaps they do not rise to the level of something he should be blamed for. This is a question of degree—of how much perfection, or self-command, we can demand of each other. But this question would not even come up if the fact that these reactions are not responsive to the man's will or judgment rendered them irrelevant to moral assessment.[65]

This is even clearer when we shift from the case of moral relations between strangers to more intimate relationships. What we hope for in our friends is that affection toward us, and concern for our interest, will occur to them spontaneously and not only when they see, on reflection, that these attitudes are called for. Something is lacking in a friend who is not moved by our welfare unreflectively, even if (perhaps recognizing this fault in himself) he is always moved to help us when he can because he carefully monitors himself and always does reflect about his obligations.

In moral assessment, as in these more personal relations, both reflective and unreflective attitudes matter, and persistent unreflective attitudes matter even if the person consistently rejects them on reflection. The relative significance of these different kinds of attitudes may be different in the two cases. The morality that applies between strangers, we might say, is in an important sense *about* self-regulation, and we expect it to involve checking one's immediate responses. Certain kinds of negative attitudes toward others are moral faults, but it is an important and expected function of moral awareness to control such feelings. We do not expect purity from everyone, but relations of love and friendship are another matter. It is not just that love involves a kind of concern that others cannot expect. It is also important (not just an ideal) that this kind of concern should be, to a large degree, a matter of immediate and spontaneous feeling.

So the relative significance of spontaneous response and reflective judgment is different in the two cases. Given the importance of spontaneous reactions in the case of friendship, however, it would be odd to say that unreflective reactions matter less in moral assessment *because* they do not fully belong to the person. Therefore, if these reactions are less significant for moral assessment than reflective judgments are, this is not because they are not attributable to the person in the relevant sense, but rather because they are beyond the kind of concern that we can demand of strangers. Their lesser significance is, as I said above, a substantive question and a matter of degree.

It might be charged that I have not taken seriously

enough the implications of the possibility that my friend is just the puppet of outside forces. Surely, the objector might say, if I were to learn that a particular reaction, such as the way she responds to my arrival, was produced in her by someone stimulating her brain, this reaction would not have the significance that I normally give it. How is it any different if the control takes place at a greater distance and over a longer time?

My response is that it is very different. The fact that a friend reacts a certain way when a certain part of her brain is stimulated tells me nothing interesting about *her*. It says nothing interesting about her *in particular*, since anyone would react that way to such a stimulus, and it says nothing interesting about her over time, since I can infer nothing from it about how she feels about me or about how she will react to my arrival (without the stimulus) in the future. "Determination" by genetic and environmental factors is very different. It determines what the person as a whole is like, rather than producing reactions that may deviate from this. The fact that a tendency to have a particular reaction (a tendency to strongly like or dislike a certain kind of situation, for example) can be explained in this way does not undermine the degree to which it is part of what the person is like.

As I have said in discussing the ethics of blame, facts about the way a person came to be the way he is, such as that he has certain attitudes because he was treated terribly as a child, can modify the attitudes it is appropriate to have toward him in ways other than by qualifying the degree to which his morally deficient attitudes are attributable to him. If a person sees no reason to give any weight to the interests of others, the fact that he is like that because he was terribly abused as a child does not make it inappropriate to refuse to consider him as a candidate for trust, cooperation, or friendly relations. He remains an untrustworthy person, with whom we can reasonably refuse to enter into such relationships. As I have said, however, the fact that he "can't help" being the way he is may make it inappropriate to berate him for being that way. Moreover, the fact that he is also a victim makes it inappropriate not to have certain other attitudes toward him, such as a degree of sympathy, and a special readiness to help him in some ways. The appropriate attitude toward him is not *unalloyed* blame, even though blame—the kind of modified relationship I have described—remains appropriate.

Two Kinds of Responsibility

I have argued that blame can be appropriate for characteristics that a person could not avoid having, and that the kind of responsibility that is a precondition for blame does not require the opportunity to avoid. There is, however, another kind of responsibility that can require adequate opportunity to avoid, and it is important to distinguish the two. Considering this distinction will lead to the question of whether one can have adequate opportunity of the required kind if one's attitudes and actions are caused by factors outside oneself, over which one has no control.

In the course of an argument about how our ideas about blame should be modified if we believe that agents lack free will, and speaking as if he were still talking about this same subject, J. J. C. Smart makes the following remark:

When, in nineteenth-century England, the rich man
brushed aside all consideration for his unsuccessful
rivals in the battle for wealth and position, and looking
at them as they starved in the gutter said to himself,
"Well, they had the same opportunities as I had. If I took
more advantage of them than they did, that is not my
fault but theirs," he was most probably not only callous
but (as I shall try to show) metaphysically confused.
A man who said "heredity and environment made me
what I am and made them what they are" would be less
likely to fall a prey to this sort of callousness and indifference.[66]

Later, in the same vein, Smart considers a man "who excuses
himself for his indifference to his less fortunate neighbor by
saying, 'Hadn't he the same opportunities as I had? He could
have got on if he had acted with my drive, initiative, etc.'" Smart
then says, "There is sense in such a remark only in so far as the
contempt for laziness and lack of drive to which it gives expression is socially useful in spurring others on to display more
drive than they otherwise should."[67]

As Smart interprets the rich man's remarks, they involve
two elements. First, the rich man is expressing a negative
moral assessment of the poor, whom he blames, or holds in
contempt, for their laziness. Second, he is attempting to justify
his indifference to the plight of the poor, and to dismiss their
claims against him for assistance or better treatment, by citing
the fact that "they had the same opportunities as I had." Smart
is assuming that these two attitudes stand or fall together—
that the rich man's indifference to the plight of the poor is jus-

tified if and only if the poor can be blamed for the choices they have made.

The idea that there is a link of this kind between responsibility and blame is commonly heard in political discourse. Conservatives often say that there are two responses to social ills such as urban crime, teenage pregnancy, and drug abuse. One response is to see these as cases of people behaving badly, in which case the remedy is that they should be made to do better. The other response is to see these ills as the products of social conditions such as poverty and inadequate educational systems, in which case the remedy is to change those conditions. To take the latter approach, conservatives say, is to deny that individuals are responsible for what they do.

One also hears expressed, from the left, an attitude that is the mirror image of this one: a reluctance to criticize the poor for faults such as drug use and lack of self-discipline because it is thought that "blaming the victims" in this way would imply that "society" is under no obligation to help them, since their fate is due to their own moral failings.

Both of these views rest on a false dichotomy. It is one question whether a person can properly be blamed for what he does and quite a different question whether he is "responsible for his fate" in a sense that relieves the rest of us of any obligation to alleviate his condition. These two questions may be more easily confused in Smart's example because the laziness that he describes the rich man as holding in contempt may be thought a moral failing. But if the response, "You could have what I have if you had chosen as I did" has any force, it continues to have force when addressed to someone who is without moral fault.

Consider, for example, a woman who chose, when she was young, to pursue an ascetic life of devotion to art, and who therefore made no effort to launch the kind of career that could have led to a high-paying job. If later, when she is old and sick, she were to complain of her meager life and perhaps seek assistance, the rich man's response that she could have been much better off if she had so chosen would have at least as much force as in the example Smart appeals to. It might well have *more* force, because as I am imagining the case she really did have the choice, which the poor people in Smart's example may not have had. Whether this response has enough force to undermine her claims to assistance is a further question. Perhaps it does not. The point is just that the force of "you had the choice" does not depend on the fact that the choices made by the person in question were morally objectionable. A person can be responsible for her fate in a sense that undermines her claim on others for help without being open to moral criticism for what she has chosen.

The same is true in the opposite direction. Even if a certain problem arises from people having behaved badly, it does not follow that society is not obligated to do something about this problem. It may be, for example, that the conditions in which the people grew up, and which led them to behave in bad ways, would not exist in a decent society. So a problem can, at the same time, be both grounds for moral criticism of individuals *and* something that calls for social action.

Confusion between these claims may be invited by the fact that both may be expressed in judgments using the term 'fault': blame involves the attribution of a moral fault, and a claim of responsibility of the second kind may be expressed by saying, "It's his fault." But despite this verbal similarity, the two kinds of claims are quite distinct. The latter, unlike the former, is primarily a claim about what others owe to the person.

This distinction is particularly clear if blame is seen as simply a matter of negative moral evaluation. On this interpretation, it is clear that the kind of responsibility required for blame is what I have called "responsibility as attributability."[68] All that is required is that the attitudes that make blame appropriate can in fact be attributed to the person as "his." As I have argued, it is not necessary, in order for this to be so, that the person chose to have those attitudes, or that he could have avoided having them by choosing appropriately. By contrast, the kind of responsibility expressed in the claim, "It's your fault"—what I have called substantive responsibility—appeals to the idea that the person has had "adequate opportunity to avoid" the situation in question.[69]

As I have said, the place of this idea is in response to someone's claim that others have an obligation to provide him or her with some benefit. The response presupposes that the underlying obligation is not an obligation to provide the benefit, but only an obligation to put a person in a good enough position to gain the benefit by choosing appropriately, and the response claims that this obligation has been fulfilled.

The qualification "good enough" is important. Having "had the choice" is not an all or nothing affair. Many factors, such as available information, available alternatives, and the conditions under which the choice must be made, can affect the value of having that choice as a protection against losing the benefit. So the question is not merely whether the person could have avoided the result by choosing differently, but also whether he or she had a good enough opportunity to do so. Applying this to the case of Smart's rich man, we might suppose that he takes the poor man in the gutter to be protesting the fact that he does not have a more comfortable life. The rich man's response is, "No one is obligated to provide you with a comfortable life, but only with the opportunity to gain one by working hard. You had that opportunity, just as I did, so you can't complain." This response can of course be disputed. Even if the poor man's condition is partly the result of choices he made, one can wonder whether he was placed in sufficiently good conditions for making those choices. But the overall structure of the argument is clear, and familiar.

Blame, as I interpret it, involves more than negative moral evaluation. So my interpretation makes judgments of blameworthiness more similar to judgments of substantive responsibility than they would be according to a purely evaluative interpretation.[70] In my view, both kinds of judgments involve substantive claims about the ways we are justified in interacting, or declining to interact, with the individuals in question. But the forms of interaction that judgments of blameworthiness recommend withholding are not owed unconditionally: as I have argued, their suspension can be fully justified simply by what a person is like. Therefore, unlike judgments of substantive responsibility that might be expressed by saying, "It's your own fault!" judgments of blameworthiness, as I interpret them, need not be justified by appeal to the idea of adequate opportunity to avoid. Substantive responsibility and the kind of responsibility presupposed by moral blameworthiness thus remain distinct, and responsibility of the latter kind does not require opportunity to avoid.

Freedom and Opportunity to Avoid

Where the requirement of opportunity to avoid *does* apply, however, it may bring with it a stronger requirement of freedom, and worries about free will may be less easily set aside than in the case of moral blame.[71] The problem is obvious enough. Suppose a person complains about bearing some burden, and we reply, "You had the same opportunity to choose that everyone else had, and you could have avoided this burden if you had chosen to do so." He may reply, "What do you mean 'could have'? The way I reacted when presented with these alternatives was determined by factors over which I had no control."

This complaint might be answered by stressing that all that was being claimed was that the person "had a choice" in the purely psychological sense, in which a person has a choice whether A or B if he is put in circumstances in which whether A is realized or B is realized depends on how he responds, and he is aware that this is so. As I have said, merely "having the choice" in this minimal sense may have little or no moral significance. Much depends on the conditions under which the choice is made: the quality of information that the person has, the absence of competing pressures, the attractiveness of the available alternatives, and so on. These factors are encompassed in the idea of *adequate* opportunity to avoid, and the response of Smart's rich man is weakened by our supposition that the conditions under which the poor man chose—and might have chosen differently—did not provide him with adequate opportunity in this sense.

No matter how good the conditions for choice may be, however, there may be some people who will choose badly, with results they have good reason to regret, and we need to be able to answer their complaints. They can say, "What good did it do me that I 'had the choice' under what would, for most people, have been 'favorable conditions'? They were not favorable for *me*. And it was certain that they would not be, given the way I am—that is, given the way my heredity and environment made me."

The best response, I believe, is to say that "giving someone the choice" (under favorable conditions) is just *one* of the things that we can do to protect them against unwanted outcomes. It is not foolproof, but neither are other protections. Vaccines, for example, do not work for everyone. But from the fact that a vaccine does not work for someone, and that she therefore gets the disease, it does not follow that, in giving her the vaccine and taking other public-health measures, we have not done as much as we could be required to do to protect her against infection. If we have, then she has no complaint.

Similarly, one thing we can do to reduce the likelihood of bad consequences befalling people is to put people in conditions in which they have the choice, in the purely psychological sense, of avoiding those consequences. If the conditions are good enough (if the information and incentives are such as to be effective for most people), and if we have taken whatever further measures are required to reduce the chances of harm, then if a person chooses badly and suffers the harm, he has no complaint against us. That is to say, the result is his responsibility rather than ours, whether or not he was free in some deeper sense to choose differently than he did.

On this account, the moral significance of having a choice is merely that of being one factor that reduces the likelihood of harm. I believe that this is as much significance as choice can have, whether or not our choices are causally determined. Some people may believe that choice has greater significance than this. They believe that choice can have a special licensing power to confer legitimacy on its consequences, but that it can have this significance only if the choice is not caused by factors outside the agent. If this is the standard view, then I am content to take a somewhat revisionary view.

However, having offered a positive account, albeit a somewhat revisionary one, of how the fact that someone was given a choice could have moral significance even if choices are caused, I can follow this up with a more aggressive line. This is to ask the incompatibilist to explain more exactly what kind of freedom he believes that morally significant choice must have, and to explain how choices that were free in this sense could have a special licensing power. I do not myself see how these questions can be given satisfactory answers.

An Example: The Cosby Controversy

The points I have made in preceding sections about responsibility, blame, and the ethics of blame can be illustrated by considering a controversy generated by some remarks made by the African American comedian Bill Cosby. Speaking at an event sponsored by the National Association for the Advancement of Colored People (NAACP), the NAACP Legal Defense and Education Fund, and Howard University in 2004 to mark the fiftieth anniversary of *Brown v. Board of Education,* Cosby sharply criticized poor blacks in the United States. He criticized them for the way they dress, for their bad manners, for failing to speak proper English, for failing to apply themselves in school, and, in general, for failing to strive to do the things they would need to do in order to get ahead in American society. He also criticized African American parents for failing to see to it that their children corrected these behaviors, and he criticized young blacks for having children when they were not ready to be good parents. The black poor, he said, "are not holding up their end in this deal." As one might expect, Cosby's speech drew praise from many conservatives and outraged criticism from liberals, especially from many African Americans. I will focus here on the criticism, which will serve to illustrate a number of the points made in previous sections.

Cosby is himself very wealthy, and it is natural to interpret his remarks as having more than a little in common with those of the imaginary rich man in Smart's example. One criticism of Cosby involves the left-wing version of the common error I discussed in connection with that example. This is the error of supposing that if poor blacks were open to criticism for the faults Cosby charged them with, then they were responsible for their fate in a sense that would undermine any obligation on the part of the government, or their fellow citizens, to alleviate their condition. As I argued above, this does not follow. It is possible that many poor blacks are properly criticized for behaving in self-destructive ways and *also* that the government should, as a matter of justice, do more to improve their condition—in particular, that it should do more to ensure that people are not placed in conditions that generate this kind of self-destructive behavior.

However, given that many people accept the linkage between blame and responsibility that I have claimed is invalid, Cosby's remarks could have the effect of encouraging complacency of the kind that Smart's rich man expressed, and thus of undermining support for programs to aid the black poor. Whatever his intent may have been, Cosby might thus be open to criticism for not considering the political effects that his words were likely to have. But there are also other grounds on which his remarks might be open to criticism.

What Cosby was expressing seems clearly to be blame in the sense I have been discussing. He was speaking as a member of the black *community*, before an audience of mainly well-to-do blacks, on an occasion sponsored by organizations devoted to advancing the legal, economic, and social condition of blacks in this country. His remarks thus presupposed a certain relationship between himself, his audience, and those he was criticizing, namely the relationship of fellow members of a historically oppressed group. He can be fairly interpreted as saying that the attitudes and behavior of many members of today's black underclass impair their relationship with other blacks in a way that makes appropriate a corresponding adjustment of attitudes toward them on the part of Cosby and the members of his audience.

It is not clear exactly what adjustments in attitude he was saying are called for, but they might include at least: (1) a decrease in sympathy for the poorer members of the black community, and a decreased tendency to view them mainly as victims of unjust deprivation, and (2) a suspension of the solidarity that normally requires members of the black community to defend other members against criticism from outside the group, and to refrain from criticizing other members before an audience of outsiders. These attitudes are quite explicit in Cosby's remarks about "not holding up their part of the deal" and about his willingness to "air dirty laundry" in public. It would be a further step for Cosby to say that because "lower economic people" were failing to "hold up their end of the deal," better-off blacks and organizations like the NAACP should no longer feel obligated to work on their behalf. I do not believe that he was expressing this view, but he may have been suggesting that it was not out of the question.

Why might these expressions of blame be deemed inappropriate? It might be said that he was just expressing intraracial class antagonism—black middle-class disapproval of, and desire not to be associated with, the "lower economic people" whose uncouth dress and speech he was condemning. There may well have been an element of this in Cosby's remarks, but he also mentioned more serious matters, such as irresponsible parenting and the failure to study hard in school. If these more serious criticisms have some validity, why should it be thought inappropriate for him to make them?

One answer might be that Cosby, who was lucky and is now wealthy, was showing insufficient sympathy for the plight of the poor and for the difficulties they face. But how would this undermine blame? The idea might be that someone with a fully sympathetic understanding of the plight of poor blacks would understand that the conditions they have to struggle with should excuse them from blame even if they do not justify their conduct. But this answer seems to run the risk of denying that poor blacks are responsible agents. Another possible answer would be that solidarity requires lucky, well-to-do members of the black community, like Cosby, to be unconditionally supportive of their less-fortunate brethren, and not to take even admittedly criticizable behavior as grounds for withdrawing sympathy and support. This answer would require that the attitude of well-off blacks toward the poor should be something more like the attitudes of brothers and sisters toward one another.

So understood, the idea would be that members of the black community who now have relatively easy lives lack standing to blame those whose lives are hard. But there seems also to be something in the criticism that has more to do with Cosby in particular. It might be this: that he grew rich and famous partly through a television situation comedy that minimized the problem of race in America (and was popular in part because it did). By denying the reality of racism, and encouraging the white community to deny it, he undermined his own relation with the black poor. And having let the black poor down in this way, he is not in a position to maintain that they have, as it were, let *him* down by their failure of self-discipline.

I have not tried to assess fully the merits of these reactions to Cosby's remarks, and there are no doubt other interpretations of these criticisms that I have not considered. My purpose here has been only to show how the conception of blame that I have been advancing provides an ethical framework within which many of these criticisms make sense, and can be assessed.

Conclusion: Is My View Also Revisionary?

The claims I have made in this chapter fall into two groups. Those in the first group are analytical and normative. Employing the distinction between permissibility and meaning, I have called attention to a particular kind of moral response that has two components. The first is a judgment about the meaning of an action: that it indicates something about the agent in virtue of which certain of the agent's relations with others are impaired. This judgment depends on what the relations in question are and what they require. The second component is a decision by a person to have attitudes toward the agent that reflect this impairment. This may represent a change in the person's attitudes toward the agent or merely a confirmation of attitudes already held. The attitudes a person is justified in deciding to hold will depend not only on what the agent has done and his or her reasons for doing it, but also on the person's prior relations to the agent—relations such as friend, neighbor, coworker, victim, or someone living in a distant time and place who is not directly affected by what the agent did.

The claims in my second group are interpretive claims about our ideas of blameworthiness and blame. I said that what we normally call a judgment of blameworthiness should be understood as a conclusion of the kind just described: a conclusion that the action shows something about the agent that impairs his or her relations with others. To blame someone, I said, is to have the attitudes toward him or her that such judgment holds to be appropriate.

Even if the claims in my first group are correct, those in the second group might be mistaken: my interpretations of blameworthiness and blame may be revisionary. There are several reasons why one might think that this is so.

First, in my view, a conclusion that someone is blameworthy is a conclusion about that person's attitudes. The person's willingness to perform a certain action on a given occasion can provide evidence for this conclusion, but the conclusion is in principle one that could be reached on other grounds. It may seem, therefore, that my view fails to account sufficiently for the fact that blame is always *for* some action. I have explained above why I do not find this objection compelling.

Second, it might be held that the appropriateness of blame does not vary in the way I suggest, according to the relation between the agent and the person who is doing the blaming. Rather, it might be claimed that to blame someone is to accept a negative evaluative judgment about that person's character or moral record, a judgment that anyone can make in the same way. If there is a disagreement here, it is a disagreement about the character of our moral experience. I take it to be an advantage of my view that it accounts for what seems to me the evident variability of blame, and its clear dependence on particular relationships. This strength of the view is shown in particular in the account it offers of what I have called the ethics of blame.

Third, my account of blame may strike some as revisionary in holding that people can be blamed for things that are not under their control. While acknowledging that my view may be revisionary in this way, I want to emphasize that I did not shape my account of blame with the aim of avoiding problems about free will. My argument thus does not have the form that Nagel criticizes when he writes: "The erosion of moral judgment emerges not as the absurd consequence of an over-simple theory, but as a natural consequence of the ordinary idea of moral assessment, when it is applied in view of a more complete and precise account of the facts. It would therefore be a mistake to argue from the unacceptability of the conclusions to the need for a different account of the conditions of moral responsibility."[72]

The question I began with was how "the ordinary idea of moral assessment" should be understood. Having come up with an interpretation that seemed to me to account well for the various distinctive features of blame, I then went on to consider what reasons there might be for thinking that blame was appropriate only for things that were under an agent's control. My argument was not that we should reject the condition of control because it has implausible consequences but that we do not have good reason to accept that condition in the first place, as applied to moral blame.[73]

Many people seem to take it as an obvious truth that blame presupposes some kind of freedom, or control over the factors for which a person is blamed. It seems to me that if this is true it must be in virtue of some feature of what blame is, and that it should be possible to spell out why this feature leads to the requirement of freedom. But this has not commonly been done. I have examined several interpretations of blame, and I have identified, in the ideas of psychological accuracy and adequate opportunity to avoid, what seem to me the most plausible reasons for thinking that blame requires a kind of freedom that we lack if our actions are caused by factors outside of us. Neither idea seems to support such a requirement of freedom as a precondition of blame, as I believe we should understand it. I will be pleased if this discussion leads others to present alternative interpretations of blame, and to offer different explanations of the link between blame and freedom.

Notes
Bibliography
Index

Notes

1. The Illusory Appeal of Double Effect

1. These may correspond, respectively, to what Elizabeth Anscombe calls an agent's "intention *of* doing what he does" and "his intention *in* doing it." See Anscombe, *Intention* (Oxford: Basil Blackwell, 1958), 9.

2. This aspect of intention is emphasized by Michael Bratman. See Bratman, *Intention, Plans, and Practical Reasoning* (Cambridge, MA: Harvard University Press, 1987).

3. See Judith Thomson, "The Trolley Problem," in her *Rights, Restitution, and Risk: Essays in Moral Theory,* ed. William Parent (Cambridge, MA: Harvard University Press, 1986), 101–102.

4. Frances Kamm has suggested one explanation. There is a conceptual distinction, she says, "between doing something because it will have an effect and doing it in order to produce that effect." Kamm, *Intricate Ethics* (Oxford: Oxford University Press, 2007), 95. The idea behind the doctrine of double effect, properly understood, prohibits only the latter. In the Loop case, although the agent acts only because the train will hit the one and thus be stopped, she does not act *in order to* hit the one. Although Kamm believes that this distinction is important, she does not believe it is the proper explanation of the permissibility of switching the train in the Loop case. (See *Intricate Ethics,* chap. 5.)

5. This example is derived from one suggested to me by Thomson.

6. Judith Thomson, "Physician-Assisted Suicide: Two Moral Arguments," *Ethics* 109 (1999): 517.

7. Jonathan Bennett makes this point in "Morality and Consequences," *The Tanner Lectures on Human Values*, vol. 2, ed. S. McMurrin (Salt Lake City: University of Utah Press, 1981), 99.

8. The distinction I am making between the two uses of principles does not coincide with the distinction between first- and second-order morality as it is drawn by Alan Donagan in *The Theory of Morality* (Chicago: University of Chicago Press, 1977), 55, or by Jonathan Bennett in *The Act Itself* (Oxford: Clarendon Press, 1995), 221–224. Unlike what they call first-order morality, what I am calling the deliberative use of a principle does not *exclude* reference to an agent's beliefs, aims, or other mental states. It simply does not immediately *require* such reference, in the way that the critical application of a principle does.

9. In earlier versions of this chapter I referred to these uses as *retrospective* and *prospective*. This was misleading because, as I have pointed out above, the question of permissibility that principles in their deliberative use are supposed to answer can be asked retrospectively and hypothetically as well as prospectively. Nor is the distinction one between first-person and third-person points of view. What I am calling the critical question—whether someone decided what to do in the proper way—is a question one can ask about oneself. And one can ask the deliberative question from a third-person perspective: one can ask, of a person in a certain situation, what that person should do.

10. See, for example, T. A. Cavanaugh, *Double Effect Reasoning* (Oxford: Clarendon Press, 2006), chap. 4, esp. 134.

11. My concern is with how this principle should be understood, specifically with whether it is best understood in a way that makes the permissibility of using deadly force depend on the agent's intent. I will therefore not enter into the difficult questions about how such a principle is to be defended, such as questions about why war should entail the suspension of ordinary moral requirements, about the permissibility of entering into war in the first place, and about what constitutes "war" in the relevant sense. It might of course be maintained that the permissibility of entering into war already depends on intent: that it is permissible to go to war with the aim of self-defense, for example, but not with the aim of conquest. My response is just the one given above: the permissibility of going to war depends not on what one sees as reason for doing so but on whether there actually *are* good reasons for doing so (given what it is reasonable to believe one's factual situation to be). Of course

there is such a thing as going to war for bad reasons in a situation in which good reasons are also present. But this entails an assessment of the way the agent decided what to do (using the principles of *jus ad bellum* in what I called above their critical employment). It should not be confused with the claim (based on the same principles in their deliberative employment) that going to war under those circumstances was impermissible.

2. The Significance of Intent

1. T. M. Scanlon, *What We Owe to Each Other* (Cambridge, MA: Harvard University Press, 1998), 298.

2. What A does in these cases violates my Principles D and L. Ibid., 300–301.

3. These considerations provide an analysis of the case Mill discusses, of a tyrant who saves his enemy from drowning in order to kill him later by torture. See John Stuart Mill, "Utilitarianism," in *Utilitarianism and Other Essays*, ed. A. Ryan (London: Penguin Books, 1987), 290n. Mill observes that the difference between such an action and the action of someone who rescues a person out of duty or benevolence does not lie merely in the motive from which the agent acts, by which Mill means "the feeling which makes him will to do so." Rather, in the case of the tyrant, "the rescue of the man is . . . only the necessary first step of an act far more atrocious than leaving him to drown would have been." In my terms, there are two things to be said about the tyrant. First, the further action that he intends to perform (killing by torture) would be wrong, and he should therefore abandon the intention. Second, insofar as he has this intention, in saving the man he would be facilitating that wrongful action. What follows, however, is again that he should abandon his intention, not that he should leave the man to drown.

4. It is perhaps significant that some defenders of the doctrine of double effect may deny this distinction, or at least maintain that an action is impermissible if the agent believes (or should believe, given her other beliefs) that it is impermissible. This may derive plausibility from the idea that an agent who does what she believes to be impermissible *acts wrongly*. But this form of words slides over the distinction, which I emphasized in the previous chapter, between the critical and deliberative applications of a principle. See the discussion in Chapter 1.

5. Judith Thomson, *The Realm of Rights* (Cambridge, MA: Harvard University Press, 1990), 229.

6. Ibid., 233.

7. I say "at least in most cases" because some excuses, such as extreme fear, may extinguish fault without making what was done permissible. I am indebted to Ralph Wedgwood for helpful discussion of this point.

8. I discuss this matter further in Chapter 4.

9. Barbara Herman argues for a similar temporal extension of the object of moral assessment in "What Happens to the Consequences?" See Herman, *The Practice of Moral Judgment* (Cambridge, MA: Harvard University Press, 1993), 94–112.

10. I discuss the idea of meaning and its basis in relationships more fully in Chapters 3 and 4.

11. There can be an important difference between acting on one reason and acting on another when these reasons correspond to two different objectives that the act might achieve, and these objectives dictate different ways of carrying out the act. In such a case one needs to decide which reason will be the guiding one. But I don't see a similar possibility in cases that do not require a choice between different courses of action.

12. This is not to say that permissibility applies only to actions that an agent actually does choose. One can do something impermissible without realizing it (for example, through negligence). What is impermissible in such a case is acting without due care, care that one could have taken even if one did not choose not to.

13. For related discussion see Pamela Hieronymi, "Controlling Attitudes," *Pacific Philosophical Quarterly* 87, no. 1 (March 2006): 45–74.

14. Christine Korsgaard makes a similar point in the chapter "Kant's Formula of Universal Law," in Korsgaard, *Creating the Kingdom of Ends* (Cambridge: Cambridge University Press, 1996), 84.

15. On this account, the realm of permissibility would seem to correspond to what Kant called duties of justice as opposed to duties of virtue. Kant says that duties of justice are distinguished by being duties that a person can be coerced to fulfill. Immanuel Kant, *Metaphysics of Morals*, trans. Mary Gregor (Cambridge: Cambridge University Press, 1991), 188, *Ak.* 383. If one can be coerced to do only those things one can choose to do, then the range of permissibility would seem to correspond to the range of things that could be the objects of duties of justice in Kant's sense. There is, however, another limit on coercion. One can be coerced to adopt a certain end. If a gangster tells me that if anything happens to his girlfriend while he is in jail I will die a painful death, I may

acquire the end of keeping her safe and pure. But one cannot be coerced to adopt an *ultimate* end; if, as in the gangster case, one adopts an end for some further reason, it is not one of one's own ultimate ends. I suspect that it may be this limitation, rather than the one based on choice, that Kant had in mind.

16. The argument here has the same structure as the one I discussed above in considering the case for therapeutic cloning.

17. The following example is derived from one offered by Gerald Dworkin.

18. *Summa Theologica* II-II q.64 a.7. See Thomas Aquinas, *On Law, Morality, and Politics*, ed. William P. Baumgarth and Richard J. Regan (Indianapolis: Hackett Publishing, 1988), 225–227.

19. For ideas in the following paragraphs I am indebted to discussions with Japa Pallikkathayil. My understanding of coercion has benefited greatly from discussions with her and from her dissertation, "Your Money or Your Life: Coercion in Moral and Political Philosophy," PhD diss., Harvard University, 2008.

20. They might be called "coercive threats," but it is not clear that all such threats constitute coercion in the usual sense of that term. If I threaten to resign unless my employer increases my salary, this is an incentive threat in the sense I have defined. Whether it constitutes coercion is another matter, which I wish to avoid; hence my choice of terminology.

21. I discuss such cases in Scanlon, "The Significance of Choice," in *The Tanner Lectures in Human Values*, vol. 7, ed. Sterling M. McMurrin (Salt Lake City: University of Utah Press, 1988), 149–216, and in Scanlon, *What We Owe to Each Other*, chap. 6.

22. I discuss such differences in connection with the "symbolic" value of choice and objections to paternalism in Scanlon, *What We Owe to Each Other*, 253.

23. A counterexample would be a case in which it is permissible to make a threat that it would be impermissible to carry out (as has been claimed for a strategy of nuclear deterrence). I will not explore this possibility here since my concern is with considerations that may make threats *im*permissible.

24. The balance of reasons is different in cases in which the reason for the discretionary power in question is to give the agents an important form of control over their lives, perhaps even control over the same aspects of life that are at stake for "victims." This is the case in Nozick's fa-

mous marriage example. See Robert Nozick, *Anarchy, State, and Utopia* (New York: Basic Books, 1974), 269. He uses this example to argue in general against a "right to have a say over what affects you." But this involves generalizing from a case in which the interests at stake on the two sides are the same, to cases in which they are not. I should add that in this argument Nozick is responding to his opponents in (more or less) their own terms. In his own view, discretionary rights, such as the rights of employers, do not need the kind of justification I am here describing.

3. Means and Ends

1. I argue for a broader idea of value in Scanlon, *What We Owe to Each Other* (Cambridge, MA: Harvard University Press, 1998), chap. 2.

2. Korsgaard writes, "When Kant says, 'Rational nature exists as an end in itself. Man necessarily thinks of his own existence in this way; thus far it is a subjective principle of action' [G420] I read him as claiming that in our private rational choices and in general in our actions we view ourselves as having a value-conferring status in virtue of our rational nature. We act as if our own choice were the sufficient condition of the goodness of its object: this attitude is built into (a subjective principle of) rational action." Christine Korsgaard, "Kant's Formula of Humanity," in *Creating the Kingdom of Ends* (Cambridge: Cambridge University Press, 1996), 122–123.

3. I argue for this in Scanlon, "Reasons: A Puzzling Duality?" in *Reason and Value: Themes from the Moral Philosophy of Joseph Raz*, ed. R. Jay Wallace et al. (New York: Oxford University Press, 2004), 231–246.

4. Ibid. For criticism of my treatment of this case, and a stronger argument that even in this case intentions do not provide reasons, see John Brunero, "Are Intentions Reasons?" *Pacific Philosophical Quarterly* 88 (2007): 424–444.

5. Immanuel Kant, *Groundwork of the Metaphysics of Morals*, trans. James W. Ellington (Indianapolis: Hackett Publishing, 1983), 36, *Ak.* 429.

6. I consider the significance of such reasons in Scanlon, *What We Owe to Each Other*, chap. 3, see esp. 126–133.

7. This is what Parfit calls the Kantian Contractualist Formula: "Everyone ought to follow the principles whose universal acceptance everyone could rationally will." Derek Parfit, *On What Matters* (Oxford: Oxford University Press, forthcoming), section 45. Parfit's idea of what

one can "rationally will" is quite different from Kant's, as I argue in my own contribution to *On What Matters*, "How I Am Not a Kantian."

8. Scanlon, *What We Owe to Each Other*, esp. chaps. 4 and 5.

9. Parfit, *On What Matters*, section 26. I have adapted the example slightly. What Parfit says is that although the gangster treats the coffee seller merely as a means, what he does is not wrong.

10. Kant, *Groundwork*, 11, *Ak*. 398.

11. Barbara Herman, "On the Value of Acting from the Motive of Duty," in *The Practice of Moral Judgment* (Cambridge, MA: Harvard University Press, 1993), 12–15.

12. Immanuel Kant, *Metaphysics of Morals*, trans. Mary Gregor (Cambridge: Cambridge University Press, 1991), section 46, 261–262, *Ak*. 470–471.

13. Kant, *Groundwork*, 7, *Ak*. 393.

14. Immanuel Kant, *Critique of Practical Reason*, trans. L. W. Beck (Indianapolis: Bobbs Merrill, 1956), 89, *Ak*. 86. This difference between Kant's view and mine might be traced to a deeper difference in our views of reasons. I hold with Kant that the requirements of what I will call in Chapter 4 the moral relation with others are unconditional. But because of Kant's views about reasons, and the divide he sees between Reason and inclination, he believes that no requirements could have this unconditional character unless they were grounded in Reason—in our "higher nature," as described in the passage just quoted.

15. Christine Korsgaard, "The Right to Lie: Kant on Dealing with Evil," in *Creating the Kingdom of Ends* (Cambridge: Cambridge University Press, 1996), 138.

16. Korsgaard might disagree. She may believe that there is a more fundamental obstacle to willing the permissibility of such actions, which is understated, or misstated, by saying just that we have reason to object to being treated in this way.

17. Korsgaard develops a view like this in the latter part of "The Right to Lie."

18. Compare what Kamm calls "the authority over the self." See Frances Kamm, *Intricate Ethics* (Oxford: Oxford University Press, 2007), 87–89. I agree with Kamm that the basic wrong here is harmful involvement of others in one's plans without their consent, but in explaining this wrong I would not place the weight she does on ideas of "insult" and "disrespect." In my view these ideas are better understood as aspects of meaning rather than as determinants of permissibility.

19. A point made by Ralph Wedgwood.

20. Judith Thomson, "The Trolley Problem," in Thomson, *Rights, Restitution, and Risk: Essays in Moral Theory*, ed. William Parent (Cambridge, MA: Harvard University Press, 1986), 94–116; see esp. 108–111.

4. Blame

1. I discuss the difference between wider and narrower notions of morality in Scanlon, *What We Owe to Each Other*, chap. 4; see 171–178.

2. See Thomas Nagel, "Moral Luck," in *Mortal Questions* (Cambridge: Cambridge University Press, 1979), 28–29. See also Adam Smith, *The Theory of Moral Sentiments* (Indianapolis: Liberty Classics, 1969), 175–176.

3. Ibid.

4. Jonathan Glover described such a view: "Involved in our present practice of blame is a kind of moral accounting, where a person's actions are recorded in an informal balance sheet, with the object of assessing his moral worth." Glover, *Responsibility* (London: Routledge and Kegan Paul, 1970), 44. Gary Watson cites Glover and questions what the point of this assessment might be in Watson, "Responsibility and the Limits of Evil: Variations on a Strawsonian Theme," in *Perspectives on Moral Responsibility*, ed. John Martin Fischer and Mark Ravizza (Ithaca: Cornell University Press, 1993), 125.

5. This seems to be Hume's view of moral assessment. He writes, "'Tis evident, that when we praise any actions, we regard only the motives that produced them, and consider the actions as signs or indications of certain principles in the mind and temper." David Hume, *A Treatise of Human Nature*, ed. P. H. Nidditch, book 3, part 2, section 1, (Oxford: Oxford University Press, 1978), 476.

6. P. F. Strawson, "Freedom and Resentment," *Proceedings of the British Academy* 48 (1962): 1–25, reprinted in Gary Watson, *Free Will*, 2nd ed. (Oxford: Oxford University Press, 2003), 72–93. Subsequent references will be to this reprinting. Strawson does not describe reactive attitudes as forms of blame, but this identification is a natural application of his analysis.

7. Compare Joanna North, "Wrongdoing and Forgiveness," *Philosophy* 62 (1987): 499–508. "Typically an act of wrongdoing brings about a distancing of the wrongdoer from the one he has harmed. This distancing involves a forfeiting of the right to the wronged party's sympathy, affection or trust, and is felt as a breakdown or a distortion in the personal relations between the parties. This distortion may also affect their rela-

tions with other people who are not directly involved" (502–503). North does not mention blame. Her topic is forgiveness, but I take her idea to be the same as the one I am developing, since forgiveness is plausibly understood as the healing or setting aside of blame. As North writes, "Forgiveness is a way of healing the damage done to one's relations with the wrongdoer, or at least a first step towards a full reconciliation" (503). I am indebted to Stuart Robinson for calling North's article to my attention.

8. To forestall the impression that I am advocating a particularly harsh and demanding conception of friendship, I would emphasize that I am not taking a position here about which of these responses is called for in Joe's case. The point of my analogy is to draw attention to the kind of responses that blame involves. Exactly which of these is called for in any particular case is a further question.

9. I am indebted to Jeff King and David Sobel for raising this issue.

10. For this reason, 'expectation,' insofar as it suggests specifically expectations about what someone will *do,* may not be the best word. Perhaps 'assumption' might be better. But I will continue to speak of 'expectations' since this is the term that has generally been used in this context. See, for example, R. Jay Wallace, *Responsibility and the Moral Sentiments* (Cambridge, MA: Harvard University Press, 1993), 20–25. Wallace's view is like mine in its emphasis on relationships, which consist in the parties' holding each other to certain expectations. To hold someone to an expectation, in his view, is "to be susceptible to a certain range of emotions if the expectation is violated, or to believe that it would be appropriate for one to feel those emotions if the expectation is violated" (23). His view differs from mine in the emphasis it places on these reactive emotions.

11. I am grateful to Samuel Scheffler for pressing on me the need to emphasize this distinction.

12. There is also the possibility that I never had any reason to think that he was my friend: that the idea was a mistake, or a fantasy, on my part. If this were so then I would have reason to revise my intentions and expectations, but nothing analogous to blame of Joe would be involved. I am indebted to Kyla Ebels Duggan for calling this possibility to my attention. The corresponding possibility in regard to the moral relationship that is my main concern would be that I was mistaken in thinking that Joe was a rational agent at all, capable of standing in moral relations with others. In this case as well, the change in attitude that would be called for

would not be analogous to blame, because it would not be occasioned by Joe's failure to live up to the standards involved in a relationship he was a party to.

13. Norvin Richards cites what he takes to be the absence of such a relationship as an objection to the view that forgiveness is a matter of "reestablishing a relationship" with the person who has wronged us. See Richards, "Forgiveness," *Ethics* 99 (1988): 79.

14. In a somewhat similar vein, John Skorupski says that a characteristic disposition to which what he calls the "blame-feeling" gives rise is a partial and temporary "withdrawal of recognition," of those toward whom it is felt as members of the moral community. See Skorupski, *Ethical Explorations* (Oxford: Oxford University Press, 1999), 151.

15. Sara Olack defends such a view in "Punishment as Negative Reciprocity," PhD diss., Harvard University, 2006. Some of what Peter Strawson says suggests a similar view. As Strawson sees it, the appropriate reaction to violation of moral demands goes beyond reactive attitudes such as indignation, disapprobation, and resentment. These attitudes, he writes, "tend to inhibit or at least to limit our goodwill towards the object of these attitudes, tend to promote an at least partial and temporary withdrawal of goodwill." He goes on to explain this withdrawal of goodwill as follows: "The partial withdrawal of goodwill which *these* attitudes entail, the modification *they* entail of the general demand that another should, if possible, be spared suffering, is, rather, the consequence of *continuing* to view him as a member of the moral community; only as one who has offended against its demands. So the preparedness to acquiesce in the infliction of suffering on the offender which is an essential part of punishment is all of a piece with this whole range of attitudes of which I have been speaking." Strawson, "Freedom and Resentment," 90–91.

16. George Sher also holds that the morally vicious do not forfeit their rights, but that the value of their well-being and happiness is decreased. Sher, *Desert* (Princeton: Princeton University Press, 1987), 148. I will argue that the latter is not so, although we may have less reason to hope for their happiness and success and be pleased by it.

17. Strawson's claim that resentment involves "partial withdrawal of goodwill" ("Freedom and Resentment," 90–91) may gain plausibility by failing to draw this distinction. A number of the attitudes I have just listed as being withdrawn in cases of blame, such as an intention to help a person with his or her projects and a disposition to hope that things go well for him or her, might be called forms of goodwill. So in this sense I

would agree that blame involves "withdrawal of goodwill," but not that this withdrawal includes "preparedness to acquiesce in the infliction of suffering" (ibid.). Strawson's use of the term 'goodwill' bundles together a very plausible claim and a highly controversial one.

18. This means that blame, in contrast to a judgment of blameworthiness, is a second-personal attitude in the sense described by Stephen Darwall. See Darwall, *The Second-Person Standpoint* (Cambridge, MA: Harvard University Press, 2006), chap. 4.

19. Strawson also notes that different reactive attitudes are appropriate for those who stand in different relations to an action. He distinguishes between personal reactive attitudes, such as resentment, which are "essentially those of affected parties or beneficiaries," and "vicarious or impersonal, or disinterested, or generalized analogs" of these. He includes moral indignation in the latter category, and says that although one can feel indignation on one's own account it is the capability of being held impersonally or vicariously that makes it appropriate to call such attitudes 'moral.' "Freedom and Resentment," 83–84. The range of standpoint-dependent varieties of blame that I would distinguish goes beyond the two (personal and vicarious, or generalized) that Strawson mentions in his article (although he might have recognized more in a longer treatment of the subject). Moral blame is not, in my view, mainly vicarious, or generalized. What marks out some forms of blame as moral is the relationship that they are reactions to the impairment of, rather than the standpoint of those who can properly have those reactions. I am indebted to Martin O'Neill for calling my attention to these aspects of Strawson's view.

20. Recall here Hume's observation that "'tis therefore from the influence of characters and qualities upon those who have an intercourse with any person, that we blame or praise him." *A Treatise of Human Nature*, book 3, part 3, section 1, 582. See also Smith, *Theory of Moral Sentiments*, 141–142, 149. Hume makes this observation in the course of describing a process of correction through which we achieve consistency in our moral judgments of those near to us and those farther removed in time and space, and thus also consistency in the judgments of different observers. On my account, judgments of blameworthiness have this kind of consistency, but blame is, inevitably, more variable.

21. On Hume's account, moral appraisal is always this kind of impartial (approval or) disapproval. This is why he can see it as having the consistency mentioned in the previous note.

22. Nagel, "Moral Luck," 28. Nagel's claim may be not just that we

have no reason to blame D more than C (because D is no worse than C) but also that it is *unfair* to blame D more on the basis of factors that were beyond his control. I discuss this idea later in the chapter, in the section "Blame and Freedom."

23. An evaluative interpretation of blame might be extended to account for moral outcome luck in a similar way. One could distinguish between blame, which is a negative assessment of an agent's character, and the significance that people have reason to attach to this assessment, which can be affected by consequences of an agent's action that are beyond the agent's control. As Adam Smith says, "Our indignation against the folly and inhumanity of his conduct is exasperated by our sympathy with the unfortunate sufferer." *Theory of Moral Sentiments*, 191. The question to ask about such an augmented evaluative account of blame is how this increased significance is to be understood. If the answer is that it is significant for people's relation with the agent, then this account comes close to the one I am offering. It is noteworthy that Smith seems to use 'praise' and 'blame' to denote pure evaluations of an agent's character, which remains constant in moral luck cases (see p. 175). It is our reactions of resentment and gratitude that can, he believes, be "exasperated" by an action's effects. These reactions are not purely evaluative, since they involve a readiness to inflict suffering or convey benefit (138).

24. Susan Wolf identifies this tendency, to think that D should be more concerned with what he has done than C, with our approval of the "nameless virtue" of being willing to "be held accountable for what one does, understanding the scope of 'what one does' particularly when costs are involved, in an expansive rather than a narrow way." Wolf, "The Moral of Moral Luck," *Philosophic Exchange* 31 (2001): 13. She also writes that an agent's failure to have this virtue amounts to a failure to "take the consequences of his faultiness to have consequences for him, to be a significant part of his personal history" (12). This is close to what I am saying about moral luck, except that I would write "for his relations with relations with others" instead of "for him." If one understands blame (and hence guilt) in an essentially evaluative way, as Wolf seems to do, then her nameless virtue goes beyond a susceptibility to guilt and is independent of it. In my view the two are more closely linked, since both involve a concern with the significance of one's actions for one's relations with others.

25. The "apologies" one often hears from public figures do not fulfill these functions. They thus fail to be real apologies but are instead mere expressions of regret at an outcome (as in "I am sorry if anyone was

offended by my remarks"). People who issue such "apologies" fail to take responsibility for their actions in the relevant sense. Taking responsibility involves not only admitting one's causal role, and one's faultiness, but also acknowledging the significance that this fault has had for others, and the need to take steps to restore one's relations with them.

26. Something similar is true of Strawson's account: reactive attitudes such as resentment and gratitude are not evaluations. So if the standard view of blame is evaluative, then what Strawson offers is a departure from the standard view.

27. For one view of this relationship, see Tamar Schapiro, "What Is a Child?" *Ethics* 109 (1999): 715–738, esp. section 6.

28. Here is William James on a form (admittedly a strong form) of the kind of thing that blame involves, in this case being snubbed or "cut dead": "No more fiendish punishment could be devised, were such a thing physically possible, than that one should be turned loose in a society and remain absolutely unnoticed by all the members thereof. If no one turned when we entered, answered when we spoke, or minded what we did, but if every person we met 'cut us dead', and acted as if we were non-existing things, a kind of rage and impotent despair would ere long well up in us, from which the cruelest bodily torture would be a relief; for these would make us feel that, however bad might be our plight, we had not sunk to such a depth as to be unworthy of attention at all." William James, *The Principles of Psychology*, vol. 1 (London: Macmillan, 1890), 293–294. Quoted in John Skorupski, *Ethical Explorations* (Oxford: Oxford University Press, 1999), 152.

29. An objection raised by Frances Kamm and others. George Sher raises this as an objection to Hume's view. See Sher, *In Praise of Blame* (New York: Oxford University Press, 2006), 12, 30.

30. Smith, *Theory of Moral Sentiments*, 187.

31. See North, "Wrongness and Forgiveness," and Pamela Hieronymi, "Articulating an Uncompromising Forgiveness," *Philosophy and Phenomenological Research* 62 (2001): 529–555.

32. This seems to be a limiting case of blame. But even to write someone off in the sense I have in mind is not to see him as outside the range of moral subjects. He remains a person to whom various duties are owed. Compare Christine Korsgaard, *Creating the Kingdom of Ends* (Cambridge: Cambridge University Press, 1996), 200.

33. The example is adapted from Philip Pettit, "Responsibility Incorporated," *Ethics* 117 (2007): 171–201. My analysis of the case differs from his.

34. See Korsgaard, *Creating the Kingdom of Ends*, 211.

35. Hieronymi, "Articulating an Uncompromising Forgiveness." Hieronymi's condition 3 does not follow from condition 1, since it might be that what the person did was wrong but not a violation of a duty owed to you.

36. This may capture what is plausible in the claim that punishment is owed to the criminal. But two points should be noted. First, in my view, if anything is owed it is not punishment but blame. Punishment seems to be owed only insofar as one supposes that blame must involve punishment. Second, as noted in the text, it is not clear that anything is *owed*—that is, that there is any obligation here. Would the criminal have a claim against us if we failed to blame him because it was too costly, or because we were too occupied with other problems to be concerned with him? It does not seem to me that he would. What is objectionable—that is to say, blameworthy—is failing to blame him *because* we do not regard him as capable of meaningful action.

37. It is a further question whether failing to blame in these cases can be not only blameworthy but also impermissible. On the view I am offering, to blame someone involves withholding certain attitudes toward him, such as the intention to trust him in certain ways. This is something we can choose to do or not. So it is the kind of thing to which the question of permissibility applies. It is therefore a substantive moral question whether blame is sometimes impermissible. In contrast, judgments of blameworthiness may reflect decisions but are not matters of choice. Therefore they are not attitudes to which the question of permissibility applies, although they can be the subject of moral criticism of other kinds.

38. I am indebted to Samuel Freeman for raising this point.

39. This explains Gary Watson's observation that "if one shares a moral fault with another, one may feel it inappropriate to blame the other. Here the point is not that the other is not responsible or blameworthy, but that it is not *one's* business to blame. One should tend to one's own faults first." Watson, "Responsibility and the Limits of Evil," 145.

40. Recall here Hieronymi's point about the preconditions for forgiveness.

41. Note that it does not similarly undermine the appropriateness of my concluding, or even saying, that your actions are blameworthy, so long as I am consistent in admitting that the same is true of my own.

The phenomenon in question concerns blaming rather than blameworthiness.

42. See G. A. Cohen, "Casting the First Stone: Who Can, and Who Can't, Condemn the Terrorists?" *Royal Institute of Philosophy Supplements* 81 (2006): 113–136, published online by Cambridge University Press, 5 December 2006.

43. Cohen says "condemn," but I do not believe this difference in terms is significant.

44. I will say more about this in the following section, "Blame and Freedom."

45. Watson, "Responsibility and the Limits of Evil," 138.

46. As George Sher also observes. See Sher, *In Praise of Blame*, 60.

47. The requirement of psychological accuracy can be seen as providing a rationale for the claim that moral responsibility requires what John Martin Fischer calls "guidance control." See, for example, Fischer, *My Way* (Oxford: Oxford University Press, 2006), 14–28 and chap. 5. Guidance control has in turn two elements, which Fischer calls reasons-responsiveness and ownership of the mechanism (18). On the latter, see John Martin Fischer and Mark Ravizza, *Responsibility and Control: A Theory of Moral Responsibility* (Cambridge: Cambridge University Press, 1998), 230–239. Fischer holds that moral responsibility does not require what he calls strong reasons-responsiveness (that, had there been sufficient reason for some alternative course of action, and the agent was guided by the same mechanism, then he would have followed the alternative course). See *My Way*, 60–69. In holding this, he is in agreement with what I am calling the requirement of psychological accuracy. It is less clear whether that requirement would even demand what he calls "weak reasons-responsiveness."

48. Notable among those who have pointed this out is Hume. See *A Treatise of Human Nature*, book 2, part 3, sections 1, 2.

49. Ibid.

50. Galen Strawson, "The Impossibility of Moral Responsibility," *Philosophical Studies* 75 (1987): 5–24.

51. Ibid., 9.

52. There is a way of understanding heaven and hell that makes sense on the view of blame that I am proposing. On this interpretation, the justification of heaven and hell is compatible with causal determination of our actions, although it may be incompatible with divine predestination.

Suppose that one's relationship with God is the most important thing in life, and that if one has lived in the right way, then after death one will live on in fellowship with God. This is what heaven involves. But if one's actions and attitudes are such that one's relationship with God is impaired, then it is not appropriate for God to take one into His presence. God is a forgiving God. He offers us grace if we will admit our sins, repent, and accept His love. But if we have refused to do this, then it is not appropriate for Him to take us into His fellowship. For Him to do so would be like a person pretending that someone is his friend, and treating him like one, when in fact he has behaved in a way that is incompatible with friendship and has declined to renounce these faults and be forgiven. Such a person is forever excluded from God's presence. This is what hell means, according to the view I am proposing. So described, hell may be a far cry from fire and brimstone. (It seems more cold than hot.) But it sounds worse if we suppose that there is evil in the world, and that to be excluded from a relationship with God is to be left to be tormented by temptation and evil

Even augmented in this way, this conception of heaven and hell is nonpunitive. Its point is not to affect behavior, or to reward the good and punish the bad, any more than the point of friendship is to reward good friends and punish bad ones. Understood in this way, for heaven and hell to make sense and be morally justifiable, we do not need to appeal to the idea that individuals have a fair opportunity to avoid hell. God does not owe it to us, unconditionally, to accept us into fellowship with Him, or to protect us from the pain of exclusion from His fellowship. What I call a pure desert justification is sufficient.

If, however, our sinful nature and our rejection of divine grace are predestined—due to God's own decision in creating us in a certain way—this may deprive *God* of standing to blame us for these faults, for reasons discussed by Cohen in "Casting the First Stone"—even though we are blameworthy. This would undermine the justification for hell as I am interpreting it, and perhaps according to a more traditional interpretation as well. Cohen refers to this as the "you made me do it" defense. (He does not use this particular example.)

Bearing in mind this interpretation of hell, the objection that my view of blame is "too weak," because the "moral relationship" that I claim we stand in to everyone is too abstract to matter much to people, suggests one possible reason for thinking that, as is often claimed, there can be no morality without a God. The idea would not be that morality requires the sanction of divine punishment and reward, but rather that the idea of a relationship with God that is impaired by one's sins is meaningful to people in a way that a relationship with myriad strangers is not. As Lucy Scanlon has pointed out, an analogous view of political solidarity would be that the idea of one's obligation to one's fellow citizens, as free and equal participants in a just political order, is too abstract to motivate individuals to make the sacrifices needed, for example, in wartime. What is needed, it may be said, is an idea of loyalty founded on a relationship that each citizen is taken to have with the king or queen, whom they serve and who in return cares about all of his or her subjects.

My response, as I have argued above, is that the impairment of their relations with others, even strangers, is something that people do care about and are motivated by. This is shown by, among other things, the lengths to which people are often willing to go to avoid admitting that they (individually or collectively) have wronged others. The alternative that I offer to the theistic account of heaven and hell might thus be summed up by reinterpreting a line from Sartre's play *No Exit:* "Hell is other people." That is to say, hell is the relationship with other people that one creates by treating them badly.

53. This is a central element in the revisionary account of blame offered by J. J. C. Smart in "Free Will, Praise, and Blame," *Mind* 70 (1961): 291–306. But it also plays a role in more standard thinking about the topic, including common ideas of heaven and hell. In fairness to Smart, it should be noted that the second problem I go on to discuss would not trouble him, since he does not offer his account as an interpretation of our ordinary idea of blame, but rather as a substitute for it. In his view, our ordinary notion of blame is untenable because, he believes, it is committed to a "metaphysics of free will." I am offering an account of blame that seems to me to come much closer to capturing our ordinary notion, while avoiding any such commitment. Whether it, too, is revisionary is a question I will return to at the end of this chapter.

54. Gary Watson argues that blame is appropriate only for agents who are capable of understanding the basic demand of morality, that one have a reasonable regard for others. He writes, "Since the reactive attitudes involve this demand, they are not (as fully) appropriately directed to those who do not fully grasp the terms of the demand." And, "The reactive attitudes are incipiently forms of communication, which make sense only on the assumption that the other can comprehend the message." Watson, "Responsibility and the Limits of Evil," 127. In my view, however, blame itself—the revision of one's attitudes toward a person in response to attitudes expressed in his behavior—is not, even incipiently,

a form of communication. Expressions of blame are forms of communication, and they may be pointless if the person cannot appreciate their force. But this does not, in my view, make blame itself inappropriate.

55. This broad understanding of desert-based views is in accord with Joel Feinberg's analysis of the concept of desert in "Justice and Personal Desert," in Feinberg, *Doing and Deserving* (Princeton: Princeton University Press, 1970), 55–87. He writes that "the kind of propriety characteristic of personal desert is not only to be contrasted . . . with qualification under a rule or regulation; it is also to be likened to, or even identified with, a kind of 'fittingness' between one person's actions or qualities and another person's responsive attitudes" (82).

56. Scanlon, *What We Owe to Each Other*, 274.

57. Similarly, Feinberg says that his view of desert "suggests in turn that responsive attitudes are the basic things persons deserve and that 'modes of treatment' are deserved only in a derivative way, insofar perhaps as they are the natural or conventional means of expressing the morally fitting attitudes." Feinberg, *Doing and Deserving*, 82.

58. George Sher also notes the normative weakness of an unspecified notion of what is fitting. See Sher, *Desert*, 114. In the case of moral desert, he proposes to remedy this lack by appealing to the idea that the distinctive value of persons derives from their being seekers of value, who thereby confer value on the objects of their pursuit. Because the virtuous seek value to a greater degree than others, they are themselves more valuable and confer greater value on what they seek. It is therefore appropriate that happiness be apportioned to virtue because the happiness of the virtuous is more valuable than that of others, and that of the vicious, correspondingly, of lesser value. Ibid., 144–149. Compare Robert Nozick, *Philosophical Explanations* (Cambridge, MA: Harvard University Press, 1981), 612. My view differs from Sher's and Nozick's in grounding the normative force of "appropriateness" in reasons internal to certain relationships, rather than in an idea of value that, like Kant's idea of moral worth, is open to interpretation in a more impersonal way as something that it is good to have in the world. Darwall draws a similar contrast in *The Second-Person Standpoint*, 68.

59. Thus Bernard Williams criticizes what he calls "morality" or "the blame system" on the ground that "there is a pressure within it to require a voluntariness that will be total and will cut through character and psychological determination, and allocate blame and responsibility on the ultimately fair basis of the agent's own contribution, no more and no less. It is an illusion to suppose that this demand can be met (as op-

posed to the less ambitious requirements of voluntariness that take character largely as given)." Williams, *Ethics and the Limits of Philosophy* (Cambridge, MA: Harvard University Press, 1985), 194. I agree with Williams that this is an illusion, and I am offering an interpretation of morality, and blame, that requires only this "less ambitious" form of voluntariness.

60. As Nagel writes, if we apply consistently the idea that people can be blamed only for things that are under their control, then "the area of genuine agency, and therefore of legitimate moral judgment, seems to shrink under this scrutiny to an extensionless point." Nagel, "Moral Luck," 35. The conclusion he intends to draw from this, however, is different from the one I am arguing for. The problem here is what Robert Kane calls the "intelligibility question"—that is, the intelligibility of the idea that we are ultimately responsible for our actions. See Kane, *The Significance of Free Will* (New York: Oxford University Press, 1996), esp. 13–16, 81–88. For Kane's response to this question, see chaps. 7–9. I am arguing that ultimate responsibility of this kind is not required for moral responsibility, but I should note that Kane is at least as much concerned with the threat that determinism poses to an agent's view of him- or herself. Nomy Arpaly also emphasizes this threat in *Merit, Meaning and Human Bondage* (Princeton: Princeton University Press, 2006). This problem, which I have called the personal problem of free will, may be more intractable than that of explaining why ultimate responsibility is not a precondition for moral blame. See Scanlon, "The Significance of Choice," in *The Tanner Lectures in Human Values,* vol. 7, ed. Sterling M. McMurrin (Salt Lake City: University of Utah Press, 1988), 149–216. But incompatibilist responses to the two problems are equally threatened by the question of intelligibility.

61. Saul Smilansky states this point forcefully: "Together with the moral obligation to respect and to track (in our own reactions and practices) identity, choice, and responsibility, we must also not forget the ultimate *arbitrariness* of it all. People can often be adequately characterized as *victims* of the internal and external circumstances that made them what they are—circumstances ultimately beyond their control, which they lacked real ability and opportunity to alter. Such circumstances, which lie behind their choices and their ensuing fate, are in a deep sense not their fault." "Free Will and Respect for Persons," *Midwest Studies in Philosophy* 29 (2005): 256. In my view, the idea that someone is a "victim" can be understood in three ways. First, the fact that a person's formative circumstances were very bad can change our relationship with him, as I

indicate in discussing the case of the killer Robert Harris. Second, the belief that even if our external circumstances have been entirely favorable we are nonetheless trapped by them because they affect us in ways over which we have no control may invoke the idea of psychological (or metaphysical) accuracy—that we cannot be blamed for our psychological traits because they are forced on us by our circumstances and therefore do not reflect the way "we" really are. As I argue in the text, this seems to me to depend on an incoherent idea of what "we" are really like. Third, the belief that we are trapped by our circumstances may be an appeal to the idea that we do not have adequate opportunity to avoid being the way we are. In my view, this does not apply in the case of moral blame, where opportunity to avoid is not required. Where it does apply, this worry is more serious, as I argue in the next section. Even when our practices of holding people responsible for their choices can be justified, however, the sense of arbitrariness that Smilansky describes remains relevant, as I say in *What We Owe to Each Other*, 294.

62. This seems at base to be a version of what I called above the requirement of psychological accuracy. But since it has a distinctive rationale, it merits separate discussion.

63. George Sher also argues against the idea that "no one deserves blame for anything that is beyond his control." See Sher, *In Praise of Blame*, 55–70.

64. Nagel suggests this in "Moral Luck," 32–33.

65. I argue for this point, and the one made in the following paragraph, in "Reasons and Passions," in *Contours of Agency*, ed. Sarah Buss and Lee Overton (Cambridge, MA: MIT Press, 2002), 165–183. I am indebted here to discussion with Angela Smith. See her "Agency, Attitude, and Responsibility," PhD diss., Harvard University, 1999, and "Responsibility for Attitudes: Activity and Passivity in Mental Life," *Ethics* 115 (2005): 236–271.

66. Smart, "Free Will, Praise, and Blame," 291–292.

67. Ibid., 305.

68. See Scanlon, *What We Owe to Each Other*, 248–249, 277–294.

69. Ibid., 248–249, 256–267.

70. And more similar than I suggested in *What We Owe to Each Other*, 248–249, 290–294.

71. The idea that moral responsibility requires adequate opportunity to avoid may be what tempts some to think that it calls for what Fischer terms "regulative control" rather than merely "guidance control,"

which is supported by the requirement of psychological accuracy. See Fischer, *My Way*, 14–28, chap. 5.

72. Nagel, "Moral Luck," 27.

73. Nagel considers three forms of moral luck: (1) luck in the outcome of one's action, (2) luck in the character that one has, and (3) luck in the circumstances in which one is placed. He sees all three as cases in which the judgments of blameworthiness that we are inclined to make conflict with the condition of control: "that people cannot be morally assessed for what is not their fault, or for what is due to factors beyond their control." Ibid., 25. I see these three cases as different. With respect to the first, taking into account the significance of blame as well as the quality of an agent's character, one could explain how the outcomes of agents' actions could make a difference in the attitudes it was reasonable to have toward them. With respect to the second, the condition of control lacks justification. Nagel cites examples of the third case: "Someone who was an officer in a concentration camp might have led a quiet and harmless life if the Nazis had never come to power in Germany. And someone who led a quiet and harmless life in Argentina might have become an officer in a concentration camp if he had not left Germany for business reasons in 1930" (26).

The question that these cases raise for my view is, when do hypothetical truths about what a person would do under one set of circumstances make a difference to his relationships with people under some other set of circumstances? It seems possible that if these tendencies are entirely submerged, and make no difference in what a person does or thinks or feels, then they make no difference, and blame is appropriate only under the circumstances in which these tendencies are in some way active. However, it could well be that the opportunism, cruelty, or excessive deference to authority that would have led a person to behave terribly under the Nazi regime, for example, was also very much a part of his personality in ordinary times. In that case, this fault would impair his relations with others in both sets of circumstances, although its significance would vary in the way I described in discussing blame for the outcome of one's actions. There is also, of course, the epistemological fact that it is very difficult to know what a person would do under circumstances in which he has never been placed.

Bibliography

Anscombe, Elizabeth. *Intention*. Oxford: Basil Blackwell, 1958.

Aquinas, Thomas. *On Law, Morality, and Politics*. Edited and with an introduction by William P. Baumgarth and Richard J. Regan. Indianapolis: Hackett Publishing, 1988.

Arpaly, Nomy. *Merit, Meaning and Human Bondage*. Princeton: Princeton University Press, 2006.

Bennett, Jonathan. *The Act Itself*. Oxford: Clarendon Press, 1995.

———. "Morality and Consequences." In *The Tanner Lectures on Human Values*, vol. 2, edited by Sterling M. McMurrin, 46–116. Salt Lake City: University of Utah Press, 1981.

Bratman, Michael. *Intention, Plans, and Practical Reasoning*. Cambridge, MA: Harvard University Press, 1987.

Brunero, John. "Are Intentions Reasons?" *Pacific Philosophical Quarterly* 88 (2007): 424–444.

Cavanaugh, T. A. *Double Effect Reasoning*. Oxford: Clarendon Press, 2006.

Cohen, G. A. "Casting the First Stone: Who Can, and Who Can't, Condemn the Terrorists?" *Royal Institute of Philosophy Supplements* 81 (2006): 113–136. Published online by Cambridge University Press, 5 December 2006.

Darwall, Stephen. *The Second-Person Standpoint.* Cambridge, MA: Harvard University Press, 2006.

Donagan, Alan. *The Theory of Morality.* Chicago: University of Chicago Press, 1977.

Feinberg, Joel. *Doing and Deserving.* Princeton: Princeton University Press, 1970.

Fischer, John Martin. *My Way.* Oxford: Oxford University Press, 2006.

Fischer, John Martin, and Mark Ravizza. *Responsibility and Control: A Theory of Moral Responsibility.* Cambridge: Cambridge University Press, 1998.

Glover, Jonathan. *Responsibility.* London: Routledge and Kegan Paul, 1970.

Herman, Barbara. *The Practice of Moral Judgment.* Cambridge, MA: Harvard University Press, 1993.

Hieronymi, Pamela. "Articulating an Uncompromising Forgiveness." *Philosophy and Phenomenological Research* 62 (2001): 529–555.

———. "Controlling Attitudes." *Pacific Philosophical Quarterly* 87, no. 1 (March 2006): 45–74.

Hume, David. *A Treatise of Human Nature,* edited by P. H. Nidditch. Oxford: Oxford University Press, 1978.

Kamm, Frances. "The Doctrine of Triple Effect and Why an Agent Need Not Intend the Means to His End." *Aristotelian Society Supplementary Volume* 74 (2000): 21–39.

———. *Intricate Ethics.* Oxford: Oxford University Press, 2007.

Kane, Robert. *The Significance of Free Will.* New York: Oxford University Press, 1996.

Kant, Immanuel. *Critique of Practical Reason,* translated by L. W. Beck. Indianapolis: Bobbs Merrill, 1956.

———. *Groundwork of the Metaphysics of Morals,* translated by James W. Ellington. Indianapolis: Hackett Publishing, 1983.

———. *Metaphysics of Morals,* translated by Mary Gregor. Cambridge: Cambridge University Press, 1991.

Korsgaard, Christine. *Creating the Kingdom of Ends.* Cambridge: Cambridge University Press, 1996.

Mill, John Stuart. *Utilitarianism and Other Essays,* edited by A. Ryan. London: Penguin Books, 1987.

Nagel, Thomas. *Mortal Questions.* Cambridge: Cambridge University Press, 1979.

North, Joanna. "Wrongdoing and Forgiveness." *Philosophy* 62 (1987): 499–508.

Nozick, Robert. *Anarchy, State, and Utopia.* New York: Basic Books, 1974.

———. *Philosophical Explanations.* Cambridge, MA: Harvard University Press, 1981.

Parfit, Derek. *On What Matters.* Oxford: Oxford University Press, forthcoming.

Pettit, Philip. "Responsibility Incorporated." *Ethics* 117 (2007): 171–201.

Richards, Norvin. "Forgiveness." *Ethics* 99 (1988): 77–97.

Scanlon, T. M. "How I Am Not a Kantian." In Parfit, *On What Matters.*

———. "Reasons and Passions." In *Contours of Agency,* edited by Sarah Buss and Lee Overton, 165–183. Cambridge, MA: MIT Press, 2002.

———. "Reasons: A Puzzling Duality?" In *Reason and Value: Themes from the Moral Philosophy of Joseph Raz,* edited by R. Jay Wallace et al., 231–246. Oxford: Oxford University Press, 2004.

———. "The Significance of Choice." In *The Tanner Lectures in Human Values,* vol. 7, edited by Sterling M. McMurrin, 149–216. Salt Lake City: University of Utah Press, 1988.

———. *What We Owe to Each Other.* Cambridge, MA: Harvard University Press, 1998.

Schapiro, Tamar. "What Is a Child?" *Ethics* 109 (1999): 715–738.

Sher, George. *Desert.* Princeton: Princeton University Press, 1987.

———. *In Praise of Blame.* New York: Oxford University Press, 2006.

Skorupski, John. *Ethical Explorations*. Oxford: Oxford University Press, 1999.

Smart, J. J. C. "Free Will, Praise, and Blame." *Mind* 70 (1961): 291–306.

Smilansky, Saul. "Free Will and Respect for Persons." *Midwest Studies in Philosophy* 29 (2005): 248–261.

Smith, Adam. *The Theory of Moral Sentiments*. Indianapolis: Liberty Classics, 1969.

Smith, Angela. "Agency, Attitude, and Responsibility." PhD dissertation. Harvard University, 1999.

———. "Responsibility for Attitudes: Activity and Passivity in Mental Life." *Ethics* 115 (2005): 236–271.

Strawson, Galen. "The Impossibility of Moral Responsibility." *Philosophical Studies* 75 (1987): 5–24.

Strawson, Peter F. "Freedom and Resentment." *Proceedings of the British Academy* 48 (1962): 1–25. Reprinted in Gary Watson, ed., *Free Will*, 2nd ed. Oxford: Oxford University Press, 2003.

Thomson, Judith. "Physician-Assisted Suicide: Two Moral Arguments." *Ethics* 109 (1999): 497–518.

———. *The Realm of Rights*. Cambridge, MA: Harvard University Press, 1990.

———. *Rights, Restitution, and Risk: Essays in Moral Theory*, edited by William Parent. Cambridge, MA: Harvard University Press, 1986.

Wallace, R. Jay. *Responsibility and the Moral Sentiments*. Cambridge, MA: Harvard University Press, 1993.

Watson, Gary. "Responsibility and the Limits of Evil: Variations on a Strawsonian Theme." In *Perspectives on Moral Responsibility*, edited by John Martin Fischer and Mark Ravizza. Ithaca: Cornell University Press, 1993.

Williams, Bernard. *Ethics and the Limits of Philosophy*. Cambridge, MA: Harvard University Press, 1985.

Wolf, Susan. "The Moral of Moral Luck." *Philosophic Exchange* 31 (2001): 4–19.

Index

Adequate opportunity to avoid,
179, 180–184, 185, 186, 190,
192, 198, 204–206
Agent versus action, assessment
of, 20–21, 23–24, 27
Anscombe, Elizabeth, 217n1
Aquinas, Thomas, 66
Arpaly, Nomy, 235n60

Bennett, Jonathan, 218n8
Blame, 122–214; for actions,
157–158, 159; and apology,
150–151; and blameworthi-
ness, 145, 158, 178, 179; and
character assessment,
126–127, 153–154; of children,
156; and choice, 183, 184,
190–193; and coercion,
180–181; of collective agents,
161–165; and control, 123,
149–150, 179, 194, 197–198,
212–213; and desert, 184, 188,
189, 190; as disapproval, 146,
182, 185; ethics of, 147,
166–179; as expression of
moral emotion, 6; expres-
sions of, 187–188; and
freedom, 6, 123, 179–198,
213–214; and friendship,
173–174, 189; and gratitude,
151–152; and impairment of
relations, 122–123, 128–138,
211–212; justification for, 186,
188, 189, 190; and meaning,
122, 145–146, 147–148,
159–160; and moral luck,
149–150; as negative
evaluation, 6, 122, 123, 127,
146, 150, 151, 173, 185, 186, 199,
202, 203; and praise, 151; and
punishment, 122, 230n36;
qualification of, 171–173; and
reasons, 127, 152–153, 173,
180; rejection of, 167–169;
and resentment, 127–128, 137,
143, 173; and responsibility,
123, 198–204, 208; as
sanction, 6, 184, 185–186; of

Blame *(continued)*
    self, 143, 154–155, 166; and
    shared commitment to a
    cause or value, 155–156,
    173–174; standing to, 6, 123,
    170, 175–179, 210, 231n52; and
    victim, 146, 169, 170, 171, 172,
    174; weight of, 127
Blameworthiness, 6, 131; and
    blame, 145, 158, 178, 179; and
    coercion, 181; defined, 128; for
    failure to blame, 170; as
    impersonal judgment, 175;
    and intention, 124–125; of
    past agents, 146; and reasons,
    124–125, 152–153; of self,
    154–155
Bratman, Michael, 217n2
Brunero, John, 222n4

Categorical imperative, 98,
    101–102
Causal determination, 181–182,
    192, 197
Character, 21, 126–127, 153–154,
    188, 190–193
Children, 139, 156, 171–173, 174,
    178–179, 197–198
Choice: and adequate opportunity
    to avoid, 204–206; of aims,
    59–60; and attitudes, 194; and
    blame, 183, 184, 190–193; of
    one's character, 190–193; and
    permissibility, 58–62, 88; of
    reasons, 59–62, 193–194; and
    responsibility, 201, 202–203;
    and threats, 76, 77–78, 82;
    and value of ends, 92–94, 96
Coercion, 74, 78, 108–110, 111,
    180–181, 182, 220n15, 221n20

Cohen, G. A., 177, 178
Compatibilism, 181
Consent, 6, 81, 82–83, 107–111, 118,
    119, 120
Consequences: and attempts,
    45–46; and blame, 125;
    intended versus foreseen,
    10–11, 18, 20; and intention,
    12, 13, 30–32; and reasons, 87
Consequentialism, 96–97
Contractualism, 98, 99, 100, 106
Control, 84, 85, 86, 87, 123,
    149–150, 193, 194, 196,
    197–198, 204, 212–213
Cosby, Bill, 206–210

Darwall, Stephen, 227n18
Deception, 38–39, 40, 108–110, 116
Desert, 184, 188–190
Donagan, Alan, 218n8
Double effect, doctrine of, 2–3,
    20–28, 29, 66, 87; defined,
    1–2, 14

End-in-itself, treatment as, 4–5,
    89, 91–98, 99, 117
Expectation cases, 40, 59, 62, 87
Expression cases, 39–40, 52, 53,
    57, 59, 62, 87

Facilitation, of other wrongs,
    42–44
Fault, 47, 49–50, 58, 150–151,
    154–155, 201–202
Feinberg, Joel, 234nn55,56
Fischer, John Martin, 231n47
Forgiveness, 160, 168–169
Freedom, 6, 123, 179–198,
    204–206, 213–214
Free will, 6, 198, 204

Friendship, 132–133, 134; and
blame, 173–174, 189; and
hopes, 132, 140, 144–145, 187;
impaired, 134–137, 141–142,
143, 144; and moral duty, 104;
and moral relationships, 143;
mutuality in, 133; and
reasons, 103; and spontaneity
of attitudes, 195, 196. See also
Relationships

Glover, Jonathan, 224n4
God, 183, 231n52
Gratitude, 151–152
Guilt, 143, 157, 174–175

Harris, Robert, 178–179
Hell, 183, 184, 231n52
Herman, Barbara, 104, 220n9
Hieronymi, Pamela, 168, 169
Human rights, violation of, 169
Hume, David, 158, 181–182, 185,
224n5, 227nn20,21; on liberty
of indifference and liberty of
spontaneity, 182, 192
Hypocrisy, 40, 57, 59, 174, 176

Indignation, 127–128
Intention: as aim/objective, 10, 11,
12; apparent significance of,
12–20; and attempts, 45–46;
and claims of agents, 62–69;
and claims of others, 69–74;
and expectation cases, 40;
and good action, 24, 25; and
larger course of action,
41–44; and negligence, 55;
predictive significance of, 13,
30, 43, 45, 62, 63–64, 67–68;
and reasons, 10–11, 12; and

self-defense, 66–69; and
threats, 74–87. See also
Double effect, doctrine of

James, William, 229n28

Kamm, Frances, 217n4, 223n18
Kane, Robert, 235n60
Kant, Immanuel, 5, 89, 90, 92, 93,
94, 97, 98, 99, 100–105, 106,
220n15; Critique of Practical
Reason, 105; Groundwork,
104–105
Korsgaard, Christine, 107–108,
109, 110, 222n2

Meaning, 4–7, 52–56, 87–88; and
blame, 122, 145–146, 147–148,
159–160; and Kant's idea of
moral worth, 101, 102–104;
and offers, 79–80; and
permissibility, 4, 53, 55,
62–69, 87–88, 99–105,
117–118, 211; of racial
discrimination, 73; and
reactions of others, 53; and
threats, 76, 77–78, 79, 86; and
treatment as means, 5, 6, 113,
115–117, 118
Means, treatment as, 4–5, 89,
106–117; and meaning, 5, 6,
113, 115–117, 118; in trolley
cases, 91, 119, 120; and value,
91–92
Mill, John Stuart, 219n3
Moral deficiency, 142–143, 144
Moral duty, 90, 101, 102, 103,
104–105, 106, 144
Moral grades, 127, 128, 143, 146,
153, 167, 185

Moral luck, 148–150, 237n73; and objective stigma, 125, 148; outcome luck, 126, 127, 128, 159, 228n23
Moral principles: as available to any agent, 61–62; critical use of, 3, 22–24, 26–27, 30, 32, 36, 87; deliberative use of, 2, 22–24, 26–27, 30, 32, 36, 46, 49, 56, 87; exceptions to, 21–22, 25–26, 27, 28, 33–36; as guiding agents, 50
Moral record, 126
Moral relationships, 139–152
Moral worth, 101, 102–104
Mutuality, 133, 140, 141, 142, 151, 176

Nagel, Thomas, 125–126, 127, 149–150, 213, 235n60, 237n73
Negligence, 55, 125–126
North, Joanna, 224n7
Nozick, Robert, 221n24, 234n58

Objective ought, 47–52
Objective stigma, 125, 148
Olack, Sara, 226n15

Parent-child relationship, 139, 171–173, 174
Parfit, Derek, 98, 99–100, 222n7
Permissibility: and blame, 122, 152; and choice, 58–62, 88; and coercion, 108–109, 181; and facilitation of other wrongs, 42–44; and fault, 49–50; and objective ought, 47–52; and reasons, 23, 46, 52–58, 62–69, 88, 100, 105, 115; of right actions for wrong reasons, 56–58, 88; of self-defense,

66–69; and threats, 74–87; and treatment as means versus ends, 5, 89–90, 99
Praise, 151, 152
Promises, 22, 23–24, 27, 65–66
Proportionality, 28, 67–69
Psychological accuracy, requirement of, 179, 180–183, 185, 190, 192–193

Racism, 69–74, 195
Rational beings, 89, 93, 96–97, 99, 140; as legislating, 97, 98
Reason(s): action for wrong, 56–62; and blame, 127, 152–153, 173, 180; and blameworthiness, 124–125, 152–153; and categorical imperative, 102; and choice, 55–56, 59–62, 193–194; and claims of others, 69–74; creation of by adopting ends, 94; multiple, 55–56, 102, 104; responsibility for, 60
Relationships, 128–131, 211; impairment of, 6, 122–123, 134–137, 141–145, 155, 157, 160, 169, 176, 187, 211; moral, 139–141; normative ideals of, 133–134; personal, 131–138. See also Friendship
Resentment, 127–128, 137, 143, 173
Responsibility: and blame, 123, 179–197; and coercion, 180–181; and opportunity to avoid, 204–206; for reasons, 60; two kinds of, 198–204
Retributivism, moral, 142, 145, 189, 190
Richards, Norvin, 226n13

Self-defense, 66–69, 142
Sher, George, 226n16, 234n58, 236n63
Skorupski, John, 226n14
Smart, J. J. C., 198–199, 200, 203, 204, 207, 208, 233n53
Smilansky, Saul, 235n61
Smith, Adam, 158, 228n23
Strawson, Galen, 182, 190, 191
Strawson, Peter, 127–128, 226nn15,17, 227n19, 229n26

Terrorists, blame of, 178
Thomson, Judith, 2, 18, 20, 27, 28–29, 31, 47–49, 51, 120
Threats, 74–87

Trust, 161, 162, 163, 164, 166, 187, 189
Twain, Mark, *Huckleberry Finn*, 158

Value, 91–93, 104–105

Wallace, R. Jay, 225n10
War, permissibility of bombing in, 2, 19–20, 28–32, 36, 68
Watson, Gary, 178–179, 224n4, 230n39, 233n54
Williams, Bernard, 234n59
Wolf, Susan, 228n24